Table of Contents

Chapter 1
Introduction:

In 1971 Orlando was put on the map as the theme park destination capital of the world with the opening of Walt Disney World and Magic Kingdom Park – it was a place where families could visit and dreams came true every day, and it was dozens of times bigger than its Anaheim counterpart. Much like Disney, in 1990, Universal thought it would get in on the thrill game too by opening its own East-coast theme park, similar to that which it had opened in 1965 in Hollywood but on a bigger scale. Universal made the announcement it would be bringing its own theme park to Orlando much to the delight of locals.

Disney soon saw that this new theme park could be grand competition and decided that it too would build a theme park based around studios - then dubbed Disney's MGM Studios. Miraculously, Disney's MGM Studios managed to open its doors in 1989 just before the grand opening of Universal Studios Florida one year later. MGM was a rushed project and when Universal opened it blew the Disney's MGM Studios out of the water in terms of the quality and standard of attractions.

In 1995, the expansion of Universal truly began as the company invested billions of dollars to create a second theme park - *Islands of Adventure*, three on-site resort hotels and an entertainment and dining district, *CityWalk*. It even expanded its original theme park with new areas – the aim was to create a multi-day destination.

On May 28 1999, *Islands of Adventure* opened to rave reviews with innovative attractions such as *The Amazing Adventures of Spiderman* and *The Incredible Hulk Coaster* winning awards year after year, even to this day. (Side note: In our opinion *The Hulk* still is the best coaster in all of Florida)

With this expansion, Universal moved into the mouse's territory - it was no longer a theme park, Universal Orlando became a veritable destination - a place to spend multiple days on-site, to explore themed adventures and to create memories that lasta lifetime.

The Universal Orlando Resort has in recent years become *the* theme park to visit in Orlando - the opening of innovative attractions and lands such as *The Simpsons Ride, The Wizarding World of Harry Potter, Hollywood Rip Ride Rockit* and *Transformers: The Ride* to name but a few have sent the visitor figures skyrocketing. Collectively, both theme parks now take in over 15 million guests a year.

The time for planning your trip to Universal Orlando has begun. As people have flocked to the resort over recent years the queues line wait times have got longer, new systems have been put in place and you always want to be ahead of the game to make the most of your vacation – you want to know before you go, you want to reduce your time waiting in line and you want to have an incredibly fun time. Which is why you have bought this guide, right?

When you finished reading this guide you will know all about your dining options, which attractions to do and which to miss, how to save literally hours in queue lines, where to stay, tips on how to save money and time, seasonal events, the future of the theme parks and about all the services the parks offer. With this guide you can do all this important research before you have even set foot into the parks - you will truly be ahead of the game.

Universal Orlando is an unforgettable vacation destination - you will make memories that last a lifetime. 2015 marks the resort's 25th anniversary and there has never been a better time to visit.

DISCLAIMER: This guide is Copyright © 2014-2015 of Independent Guides. Everything in this guide is of our personal opinion. Remember it is your responsibility to check which rides may or may not safe for you – we recommend that you read all the signs posted outside each ride before entering. It is also your responsibility to look after your children's welfare - if a ride or show sounds too scary, watch it on YouTube to get a better idea and if in doubt leave it for next time. Prices stated in this guide are approximate and may fluctuate.

Some images and trademarks: (c) Universal.

Chapter 2

Tickets:

There are a flurry of different ticket options that can be purchased for Universal Orlando. In this section we dissect them all.

Advanced Tickets

Advanced tickets can be bought by all guests from anywhere around the world. The easiest place to purchase these tickets is the official Universal Orlando website at www.universalorlando.com. There are two types of advanced tickets: single-park tickets which allow you access to one theme park per day (either to *Universal Studios Florida* or *Islands of Adventure* on any one day), or park-to-park tickets which allow you to enter both theme parks and go back and forth between them.

With multi-day single park tickets you are able to visit the two parks on separate days but you will not be able to visit both parks on the same day (in order to visit both parks on the same day you will need a park-to-park ticket) – single park tickets also do not allow you to access and ride *The Hogwarts Express* attraction which requires a park-to-park ticket.

As you will see from the prices below a single day ticket is expensive on its own, but additional days can be added on for $35 or less per day. Park-to-park tickets are $40 more expensive than single park tickets, regardless of the length of the ticket.

Child prices apply to children aged 3 to 9 years old. Children under 3 get free admission into the theme parks (proof of age may be requested at the turnstiles).

Single Park Tickets:

	1 Day	2 Days	3 Days	4 days
Adult	$96	$135.99	$145.99	$155.99
Child	$90	$125.99	$134.99	$143.99

Park-to-Park tickets:

	1 Day	2 Days	3 Days	4 days
Adult	$136	$175.99	$185.99	$195.99
Child	$130	$165.99	$174.99	$183.99

These are e-tickets that can either be picked up from will-call kiosks at the theme parks or printed at home saving you valuable vacation time of the days of your visits. Alternatively you can have your tickets shipped to you in the mail. Multi-park tickets bought online include a coupon book with $150 worth of savings. Tax is not included in the prices stated above. A Universal "convenience fee" of $2.15 for booking in advance will also be added to any booking made online in advance. Physical tickets will be shipped out via FedEx at an additional cost – we recommend you print your own tickets at home or use the 'Will Call' option to save on postage fees.

Special offer: Your 2-day ticket purchased through Universal Orlando, includes one extra day free making it a 3-day ticket. Tickets must be bought by June 7th 2015, and used in full by June 20th 2015. The offer is valid for U.S. and Canadian residents, and includes the blockout dates of December 26, 2014 – January 3, 2015. Tickets are valid for 14 days from the first use and must be used in full.

Top Tip: With the exception of 1-Day tickets (which are actually slightly more expensive to purchase online due to the convenience fee – though you will save a lot of time), all other **tickets are $20 more expensive per person at the park gates** (you will be able to see this 'gate' pricing in the next section). So book online and save yourself some serious cash and time. The 'Will Call' machines at the front of the park are only to pick up tickets so you must enter the ticket queue line to see a Team Member to buy your tickets in person from the ticket windows.

Top Tip 2: You can buy tickets at your on-site hotel; you will save $20 on your multi-day tickets compared to park prices meaning that you pay the same price as is charged online.

Top Tip 3: Universal does not have its own water park but you can add access to the great 'Wet and Wild' water park which is located just across the road. This add-on can be purchased on multi-day tickets – one visit is $35 or up to 14 days entry can be purchased for $55.

Top Tip 4: If you are enjoying the resort so much that you want to add extra days onto your ticket be sure to visit Guest Relations at the park before the last day expires. Here an extra day can be added for as little as $10 per ticket – making adding a day onto a trip very affordable indeed.

Top Tip 5: Be sure to ask your work HR department whether they are part of the Universal Fan Club. Membership is free but registration is only open to companies. HR can register by emailing fanclub@universalorlando.com - you will benefit from slightly discounted tickets and other offers.

Top Tip 6: The prices stated above are the ticket prices from the official Universal Orlando website. There are other websites and ticket brokers available that may offer tickets are further reduced prices. We recommend you thoroughly check out the reputation of the website you are purchasing from if you are not ordering from the official Universal website. Avoid auction and second-hand sales.

Gate Price Tickets:

If you do not purchase your tickets in advance, you will need to purchase them at the theme park gates – these are "gate price" price tickets and are by far the most expensive. The price of a one-day ticket is the same online or at the gate. All multi-day tickets are $20 more expensive when purchased at the theme park gates. In addition to paying over the odds, you will waste valuable vacation time by getting in a queue line when you will want to be enjoying the theme parks instead. As you have this guide and are clearly planning your Universal Orlando vacation in advance there is no excuse for having to buy a ticket at the gate.

Single Park Tickets:

	1 Day	2 Days	3 Days	4 days
Adult	$96	$155.99	$165.99	$175.99
Child	$90	$145.99	$154.99	$163.99

Park-to-Park tickets:

	1 Day	2 Days	3 Days	4 days
Adult	$136	$195.99	$205.99	$215.99
Child	$130	$185.99	$194.99	$203.99

Top Tip: A disability discount of 15% off the gate price is available meaning savings of over $30 on a 4-day park-to-park adult ticket. This is also applicable to members of the family who feel they will not be able to experience all the attractions in the park perhaps due to fear or age requirements. Tickets must be bought on the day from Guest Services. No proof of disability is required – remember this is a generous discount; please do not abuse it as it could be withdrawn at any time. For some tickets it will be cheaper to get the online tickets instead – you may also decide that even if there is an extra saving to be had, you would rather pay full price online and save time waiting in a queue line on the day of your visit.

Florida Resident Tickets:

Florida Residents can take advantage of discounts on multi-day tickets. Proof of residency must be shown when picking up tickets and/or when entering the turnstiles. Florida residents who are planning on visiting for more than 3 days in a year should also strongly consider the Universal Orlando annual passes.

A valid Florida ID must be shown for each ticket purchased. Accepted IDs are:

- Florida driver's license
- Florida state-issued ID card (must have Florida address)
- Florida voter's registration card with corresponding photo ID
- College ID from a Florida college or university with corresponding photo ID

Florida Resident Single Park Tickets:

	1 Day	2 Days	3 Days
Adult	$96	$120.99	$130.99
Child	$90	$111.99	$119.99

Florida Resident Park to Park tickets:

	1 Day	2 Days	3 Days
Adult	$136	$150.99	$160.99
Child	$130	$141.99	$149.99

The 2nd and 3rd days on Florida Resident multi-park tickets must be used within 60 days of the first use. Florida Resident discounted tickets must be purchased online in advance and cannot be purchased at the gates.

Blackout dates apply to Florida resident tickets. These are: Dec 19th, 2014 - Jan 2nd, 2015, Mar 28th - Apr 10th, Jun 13th - Aug 13th, and Dec 18th – 31st, 2015.

UK tickets:

Residents of the United Kingdom usually visit Florida for a longer period of time period than American visitors, so naturally Universal offers different and longer ticketing options. These "Universal Bonus Tickets" must be purchased in the UK before departing for the US as they are not available outside the UK.

2015 pricing for a 2-park bonus ticket with access to both Universal theme parks for 14 consecutive days is priced at £132 for adults and £122 for children.

A 3-park bonus ticket with access to both Universal theme parks (plus access to Wet 'n Wild) for 14 consecutive days is priced at £142 for adults and £132 for children.

Annual Passes

Annual passes allow you to visit the resort as often as you want (Subject to blackout dates on some passes) at a very low per-visit price. In addition, special perks are offered to passholders including discounts on dining and merchandise. There are three types of annual pass available. Discover them all below.

	Power Pass	Preferred Pass	Premier Pass
Pricing	$214.99	$294.99	$434.99
A year of unlimited park to park admission	No. Blockout dates apply.	Yes	Yes
Free self-parking (after first visit)	No	Yes	Yes
Free valet and preferred self-parking	No	No	Yes
Discounts on	Yes	Yes	Yes

theme park and special event tickets			
One Free Halloween Horror Nights Ticket	No	No	Yes
Free admission to select special events	Yes	Yes	Yes
Discounted food, merchandise and specialty items	No	Yes (10% off both food and merchandise)	Yes (15% off food and 20% off merchandise)
Discount on Blue Man Group Tickets	No	No	Yes
Free CityWalk club access	No	No	Yes
Discounts at on-site hotels	No	Yes	Yes
Universal Express Pass access (after 4:00pm)	No	No	Yes
8 bottles of free water	No	No	Yes

Prices are exclusive of tax. Prices are the same for all guests regardless of age.

Restrictions apply to some of these benefits. Premier Passholders also get up to 30% off room rates at each deluxe on-site hotel.

Top Tip: If you are visiting the resort for over 4 days it makes sense to purchase the 'Preferred Pass' for one member of your family, and regular park tickets for the others. The pass will give you food and merchandise discounts, as well as free regular self-parking, meaning it will likely quickly pay for itself.

Top Tip 2: Remember if you are planning two multi-day visits to the resort within a period of 365 days then an annual pass can be a real bargain. If you go one year in July and the next year in June, for example, then the second year's visits will effectively cost almost nothing.

Blackout dates for the Power Pass:
The Power Pass does not allow you access to the theme parks 365 days a year. These are the dates that are blocked out (i.e. the days you can not enter the parks using the Power Pass):

Universal Studios Florida:
- December 19th, 2014 - January 2nd, 2015
- March 28th - April 10th, 2015
- June 13th - August 13th, 2015
- December 18th – 31st, 2015

Islands of Adventure:
- December 19th, 2014 - January 2nd, 2015
- March 28th - April 10th, 2015
- December 18th – 31st, 2015

All dates are inclusive.

Florida Resident Annual Passes
Florida residents can get discounts on the prices of annual passes. Pricing is as follows:

Power Pass - $189.99 plus tax.
Preferred Pass - $259.99 plus tax.
Premier Pass - $384.99 plus tax.

Put simply, the features of these passes are exactly the same as the non-Florida resident annual passes mentioned above, except Florida residents pay slightly less for their passes. Proof of residency must be shown when picking up the Florida resident annual pass and/or when entering the turnstiles.

A valid Florida ID must be shown for each annual pass purchased. Accepted IDs are:

- Florida driver's license
- Florida state-issued ID card (must have Florida address)
- Florida voter's registration card with corresponding photo ID
- College ID from a Florida college or university with corresponding photo ID

Orlando Flextickets:

The Orlando Flexticket is a ticket option that allows you entry into both Universal Orlando resort theme parks as well as Sea World Orlando, Aquatica water park and Wet 'n Wild water park for 14 consecutive days – that is five parks filled with entertainment. It also includes free access to select live entertainment venues at Universal Orlando Resort's CityWalk entertainment complex (visitors must be 21 or older for some venues).

Another benefit of the ticket is that you are only required to pay for parking once each day, regardless of the number of parks visited. You will simply need to show the parking receipt from first park visited that day when visiting the other parks. Pricing for the Orlando Flexticket is $319.95 per adult, and $299.95 per child.

In addition, the Orlando Flexticket Plus option is also available which include access to the five aforementioned parks plus Busch Gardens Tampa Bay for the same period of 14 consecutive days. Pricing for the Orlando Flexticket Plus is $359.95 per adult, and $359.95 per child.

Both these Flexticket options can be purchased online from www.universalorlando.com or from a number of ticket brokers.

Chapter 3
Accommodation:

Deciding where you stay whilst on vacation is an important decision: you must consider price, availability, size, location and amenities in order to find the perfect room for you. Luckily, the central Florida area is renowned for having an incredible range of accommodation options to suit all tastes and budgets.

There are numerous nearby hotels that are not located on Universal property which are more reasonably priced than the on-site options. However, we feel that for the full Universal experience you should stay at one of the on-site hotels if you can afford the extra cost. You will be just minutes away from one of the most fun places in Orlando, and some would argue that the benefits of staying on-site more than make up for the extra cost.

The current portfolio of on-site hotels is made up of three "deluxe" hotel resorts (Royal Pacific, Portofino Bay and the Hard Rock Hotel) and a "moderate/value" resort (Cabana Bay). This range of accommodation options will be expanded in the future with a new hotel opening up in summer 2016.

General on-site hotel info:

There are many benefits to staying at on-site Universal Orlando hotels. Read ahead and find out more.

Staying at any one of the three deluxe on-site hotels will allow you to enjoy the following benefits:
- FREE Universal Express Unlimited ride access to skip the regular lines in both theme parks all day, a benefit that can be worth over $100 per person, per day depending on when you visit.

- Early Park Admission to The Wizarding World of Harry Potter one hour before the theme park opens to regular guests.
- Complimentary water taxis, shuttle buses or walking paths to both theme parks and Universal CityWalk.
- Priority seating at select restaurants throughout both theme parks and CityWalk.

Staying at the Cabana Bay Beach Resort entitles you to the following privileges:
- Early Park Admission to The Wizarding World of Harry Potter, one hour before the theme parks open.
- Complimentary shuttle buses, and walking paths, to and from both theme parks and Universal CityWalk.

In addition guests at all on-site resorts get:
- An option of a wake-up call from one of your favorite Universal Orlando characters
- Complimentary delivery of merchandise purchased throughout the resort to your hotel
- Resort wide charging privileges are available at on-site hotels. Upon leaving your credit card number at check-in, you can use your room key to charge purchases when paying, instead of using your credit or debit card. At the end of your stay you will settle the outstanding balance as one amount.
- Complimentary scheduled transportation to *SeaWorld*, *Aquatica* and *Wet n Wild*. This runs once a day from your hotel *to* these locations and then once or twice a day *from* these parks back to your hotel. The service is called Super Star Shuttle. Seats must be reserved at least 24 hours in advance - this can be done at the concierge desk.

In-room Wi-Fi access is offered at no cost to hotel guests for the "standard" level – if you require higher speed access there is a "premium" option available for $15 per day. The lobby and pool areas in all the on-site hotels have free Wi-Fi which you can access regardless of whether you are staying at the hotel.

For the deluxe hotels parking is charged at $20 per night for self-parking and $27 per night for valet parking (plus tips) – hotel guests pay full price for parking with no discounts. Day guests who park in the hotel lots will be charged according to their length of stay unless they are eating in one of the on-site restaurants where they can have their parking validated for up to 3 hours of complimentary parking. Parking charges at the Cabana Bay Beach Resort are $10 per night for hotel guests. Day guests will be charged according to their length of stay.

Refrigerators and microwaves are not included in any of the on-site hotel rooms, except Cabana Bay's suites. They can be rented for the standard rooms at the price of $15 per night each, plus tax. Those requiring refrigerators for medical conditions may be able to get a discount or the entire cost waived.

All the deluxe on-site hotels offer character-dining experiences where you have your food and selected characters visit your table for you to meet, chat with and take photographs with. At Portofino Bay this is at Trattoria del Porto, at Hard Rock Hotel this is at The Kitchen, and at the Royal Pacific Resort you will find this at the Islands Dining Room. Characters vary from Scooby Doo to Shrek and even the Minions from Despicable Me. Character dining usually takes place once or twice a week between 6:30pm and 9:30pm. Remember you can visit another resort to eat in its restaurant if there is no character dining at your resort during your stay. This applies to non-hotel guests too as the hotels dining facilities are open to everyone.

If you drive to an on-site resort hotel for a meal your parking ticket can be validated for up to 3 hours worth of three parking. Simply ask your server to validate your parking ticket.

The quickest way to get from the on-site hotels to the theme parks is the rickshaws – these are man-powered and have no set fee, simply tip what you think is appropriate ($2-$4 per person is customary).

Pet rooms are available at each of the deluxe hotels, although an extra cleaning fee is required of $50 per night, up to a maximum of $150 per room.

Kids Activities are available at the three luxury on-site hotels in the evenings for a fee so that the kids can be occupied whilst the parents get to spend some quality time together. Guests from any hotel can use the Kids Activities at other hotels. Information can be obtained from your hotel's concierge desk. Prices usually run about $15 an hour.

Although there is no onsite golf course, Universal has created the "Golf Universal Orlando" scheme that allows you to experience two nearby golf clubs – Grand Cypress and Windermere Country as part of your time at the resort. There is complimentary transportation provided both ways (subject to restrictions). Tee time reservations can be made online at www.universalorlando.com/golf or by calling the Royal Pacific Resort (who manage the golf bookings) on (407) 503-3097.

Despite the fact the deluxe hotels have fitness suites these are not complimentary for those staying in standard rooms - access to the fitness center at deluxe resorts is priced at $10 daily. Curiously, guests at Cabana Bay get free access to their on-site fitness center.

We do not recommend taking the shuttle bus from any of the on-site deluxe hotels. It will take you to the parking garage area that is still a significant distance from the theme parks. We recommend you use the river bot transportation instead.

Loews Royal Pacific Resort:

This deluxe resort is themed around a tropical paradise, with a stunning pool and its own white sand beach. Relax by the pool bar, admire the stunning theming and forget about the theme parks - this resort is the true way to be transported away from the hustle and bustle of Orlando's theme parks.

There may only be one pool at this hotel, but it is the largest in the city of Orlando. There is a kids' water play area here with canons instead of the usual water slide found at other resorts. There is also a white sandy beach area. A volleyball court can also be found just outside the pool – use of it is complimentary and a ball can be obtained from the pool towel location.

Cabanas with a TV, complimentary bottled water and sodas, a ceiling fan and fruit are priced starting at $100 per day. Cabana rentals can be made in person at The Gymnasium or by calling (407) 503-3235.

"Dive-In movies" are screened by the pool on select nights.

The Gymnasium features a variety of cardio, machines and free weight equipment. It is available for $10 per day, which also includes use of the sauna and whirlpool rooms. Club level and You First members do not pay a fee for these facilities.

One activity you might not associate with resort hotels is croquet but you can do exactly that on the croquet lawn by the Royal Tower wing of the hotel. Complimentary balls and mallets can be obtained from The Gymnasium.

On Friday and Saturday nights (and Tuesdays during the peak summer season) guests can enjoy the 'Torch Lighting Ceremony' with hula dancers and fire jugglers by the pool – there is no charge to watch this event.

An on-site coin-operated laundry is available. Prices are $3 per wash, and $3 per dryer load.

Dining:

Orchid Court Lounge and Sushi Bar – Continental breakfast, and bar with sushi. Breakfast entrees priced at $9 to $10. Bar entrees priced at $12 to $20.

Islands Dining Room – Table service dining. Breakfast buffet or a la Carte available, buffet priced at $19.50 per adult and $10 per child. All day menu entrees priced at $16 to $30.

Jake's American Bar – Bar, with light snacks and larger meals. Entrees priced at $10 to $30.

Bula Bar and Grille – Poolside bar and dining. Entrees priced at $11 to $15.

Emeril's Tchoup Chop – Signature table service dining. Entrees priced at $12 to $18 at lunch, and $24 to $30 at dinner.

Wantilan Luau – Hawaiian dinner show starting 5:00pm or 6:00pm on Saturdays (and Tuesdays during peak season), reservations required. Features a buffet including non-alcoholic and selected alcoholic drinks. Buffet priced at $63 to $70 for adults, and $35 to $40 for children.

Rooms start at 335 square feet in size with pricing varying from $229 to $374 per night plus tax for a standard room. This is currently the most affordable on-site deluxe hotel.

Dining Top Tip: Try Tchoup Chop's outside bar which serves the full menu from inside as well as cocktails. It can be a quick way to get a seat when the restaurant is busy.

Top Tip 1: If you choose to walk from this hotel to the theme parks, the distance covered will be about 1/3 of a mile.

Top Tip 2: Because of the location of the ferry terminals and its proximity to *Universal's Islands of Adventure* it is generally quicker to walk from this resort to *Islands of Adventure* than use the water taxi service. The same applies for the *CityWalk* area.

Loews Portofino Bay Hotel:

This deluxe hotel recreates the charm and romance of the famed seaside village of Portofino, Italy, right down to the cobblestone streets and outdoor cafes.

The resort houses 750 rooms, including 18 Despicable Me themed Kids Suites with a separate bedroom for the kids. Rooms start at 450 square feet in size with prices varying from $285 to $445 per night plus tax for a standard room, making this the most expensive of the onsite hotels.

On Saturdays during peak seasons there is a "Dive-In Movie" for guests to enjoy.

The hotel has 3 pools. The Beach Pool has a waterslide and is the largest and grandest of the pools. Pool cabanas are available for hire at the Beach Pool and the Villa Pool for those wanting to live the real luxurious lifestyle – these include overhead fans, a TV, and a mini refrigerator stocked with water and soft drinks, and complimentary fruit. Prices start at $75 per day. Reservations can be made in person at the Beach Pool hut or by calling (407) 503-1200 or 41745 from the in-room phone. The Villa Pool also has a Jacuzzi-style area. The Hillside Pool is the quietest and the most relaxing, with a view along the Bay.

The Mandara Spa, a brand synonymous with luxury treatments, is located by the Beach and offers a variety of indulgent experiences. The most basic 50-minute Swedish massage starts at $130, and you can expect to pay up to $595 for the "Nirvana...Bliss for a Day" experience that lasts over 6 hours. Facials, body therapies, nail services, waxing and haircuts are also available. Taxes and a 20% service charge are excluded from these prices. Any treatment purchased also includes full use of the spa and fitness facilities. A fitness day pass is priced at $10 per day for hotels guests or $25 otherwise. Spa treatment reservations can be made by calling 407-503-1244.

There is no coin operated guest laundry at this hotel. You can either use the hotel's laundry service or take your clothes to Hard Rock Hotel a few minutes away and wash them there.

In the evenings, weather permitting, the Portofino Bay Hotel piazza has live music and classical singers and guests can enjoy the Italian atmosphere.

One unique location at this resort is Family Art Photography where you can have a complimentary family photo-shoot at no charge. This can be done as a classic family portrait, poolside or even underwater. Sessions last 15 to 30 minutes. As the session is at no charge, the photo prints themselves are not cheap. Items vary from prints to canvases and even tiles. One 8"x10" print costs about $30, and four 6x6 metallic gloss finish prints will set you back $184 for example. Two 11"x14" canvases cost $194. A DVD of your entire shoot will set you back $375. Prices exclude tax. There is the option or ordering when you return home online at http://www.familyartonline.com.

Dining:
Bice – Table service gourmet dining. Entrees priced at $19 to $48.
The Thirsty Fish Bar – Bar with light snacks. Open from 6:00pm onwards.
Trattoria del Porto – Table service dining. Entrees priced at $9 to $18 at breakfast, and $9 and up for lunch and dinner.
Mama Della's Ristorante – Family style dining
Sal's Market Deli – Quick service dining. Serves sandwiches, paninis and pizzas.
Gelateria Caffe Espresso – Coffees and ice creams priced at $3 to $7.
Bar American – Upscale bar, also serves food. Open from 4:00pm to 11:00pm. Entrees $15 to $16. Small bites $10 to $14.
Splendido Pizzeria – Pizza, salads and sandwiches served poolside. Entrees priced at $13 to $18.

Reservations for table service dining establishments can be made at opentable.com.

Harbor Nights:

Four times per year, the Portofino Bay resort hosts 'Harbor Nights', a wine tasting and jazz event designed to capture the ambiance of the Mediterranean. Each event features select wines, gourmet food, live music and other live entertainment. Pricing is usually $45 per person in advance, or $55 on the door (subject to availability). A VIP seating option is priced at $75. All prices exclude tax. There is even a Holiday edition with a tree-lighting ceremony.

Top Tip: If you feel like walking, be advised that this hotel is the furthest deluxe hotel from the theme parks. We still think it is a manageable and pleasant walk being located 0.8 miles away from the parks. This is about a 15 to 20 minute walk all along a beautiful, scenic river.

Hard Rock Hotel Orlando:

You will feel like rock 'n' roll royalty with impeccable accommodation, a wealth of recreation and personal service and attention fit for an "A-List" celebrity at The Hard Rock Hotel – the place is lively, yet laid back. Rock fans will love the location where there is over $1million of music-related memorabilia. Classy, yet totally casual, this is a true deluxe hotel.

Rooms start at 375 square feet in size and are priced between $254 and $419 per night plus tax for a standard room, making this the mid-priced deluxe on-site hotel. We would argue that it is the best located and you can walk from the hotel to Universal Studios Florida in only 5 minutes.

The highlight of the hotel is the huge 12,000 square feet pool which features zero entry leveling and white sand. It even has an underwater sound system and a slide! The area also has a beach with a volleyball court and lounge chairs. There are two Jacuzzis, including one that is designated for adults only. Poolside orders from the bar are available.

Cabanas can be rented from $80 to $200 per day, depending on location of the cabana and the season. Cabanas include soft drinks and bottled water, a TV, fresh fruit, towels and a refrigerator.

One unique feature of this resort hotel is all the extra musical fun you can have – for example, DJ lessons are held daily during peak seasons in the lobby. What's more if you are a guitar fan then you will love the fact that you can rent out a Fender by AXE guitar at no extra cost during your stay, though a $1000 deposit is required.

Most nights there is a "dive-in movie" by the pool, and there are occasionally dive-in concerts too.

The resort includes a fitness center. A day pass is priced at $10 for hotels guests or $25 otherwise. Multi-day passes are also available. Club Level and All Access members do not pay a fee for these facilities.

Laundry is available on the second and fourth floors – pricing is $3 per wash and $3 per dryer load.

This hotel is the closest to CityWalk and the theme parks, being located right next door to *Universal Studios Florida* – it is only a few minutes walk to theme park fun.

Top Tip: Look for the plaques next to the musical memorabilia throughout the hotel; each of these has a unique number on it. Call (407) 503-2233 and enter the number on the plaque to learn more about the item you are looking at.

Dining:
The Palm Restaurant – Table service dining, steak house. Entrees priced at $12 to $60.
Velvet Bar – Bar with light snacks and bigger plates too. Entrees priced at $12 to $36.
The Kitchen – Buffet at breakfast. Table Service dining at lunch and dinner. Entrees priced at $11 to $37.
Emack & Bolio's – Ice creams, pizzas and small bites. Entrees priced at $9 to $23.
BeachClub – Bar and quick service snacks.

Reservations for table serving dining establishments can be made at OpenTable.com

Velvet Sessions – The Ultimate Cocktail Party
From January to October, on the last Thursday of each month you can experience Velvet Sessions. The event is described as "a rock & roll cocktail party held in the hotel's Velvet Bar and Lobby Lounge. Each "Session" showcases a different type of beverage theme for members to sip, shoot or guzzle along with fabulous and great live music from the nation's best rock bands."

Tickets are $29 in advance from www.velvetsessions.com or $35 at the door. VIP tickets are $50. Each ticket includes: Complimentary specialty drinks, finger foods and warm-up tunes, starting at 6:30pm until show time at 8:30pm. During the show and afterward there is a cash bar. After the band performs, stick around for a DJ set until 1:00am. This event is for ages 21 and over only. Past performers include: Brett Michaels, Joan Jett, The Tubes, Blue Oyster Cult, ABC and Foreigner to name but a few.

Cabana Bay Beach Resort:

Guests can now stay at the newest on-property moderate/value resort - Cabana Bay. The resort does not skimp on quality or decor because of its lower price tag. The resort is themed around the 1950's and 60's - with 900 standard rooms and 900 family suites.

Standard rooms are 300 square feet and are priced $119 to $194 plus tax per night - about half the price of the deluxe hotels. These sleep up to 4 guests. Larger family suites are available measuring 430 square feet; these are priced at $174 to $259 per night with suites sleeping up to 6 guests.

Even though this resort is significantly cheaper than the others, every room still includes a LCD TV, in-room safe, a coffee maker, an iron and a hair-dryer. Suites also include a kitchenette area with a microwave, mini-fridge and sink.

The resort does not have a sit down restaurant though you are close enough to visit *CityWalk* if you so desire. Instead the resort features a large food court and food trucks outside. In-room pizza delivery will also be offered.

Perhaps the biggest surprise is the exceptional entertainment on offer - there is a 10-lane bowling alley ($15 per game, shoe rental $4 per pair, and food is available), poolside movies and activities, and a games room. The resort will also feature two pools, a store and a fitness center, which includes both cardiovascular, and resistance equipment.

There are two pools at the resort. The main pool at 10,000 square feet has a water slide and a zero entry feature, and the smaller 8000 square foot pool also has a zero entry for greater accessibility as well as a sandy beach. The smaller pool even has a lazy river going around it spanning 700 feet. Free poolside activities happen throughout the day.

The Jack Lalanne branded fitness center on site is complimentary – making it a much better deal than at the other deluxe resorts where a per-day charge is required.

Self-service laundry is available for $3 per wash and $3 per dryer load.

Dining:
Bayline Diner – Quick service food court. Entrees priced at $7 to $8.50 for breakfast, and $6 to $12.50 for lunch and dinner.
Galaxy Bowl Restaurant – Table service dining and quick-service food available too. Open from 11:00am to 10:00pm. Entrees priced at $6 to $10.
Atomic Tonic – Poolside bar with drinks and limited snacks. Cocktails $9 to $13.
The Hideaway Bar & Grill – Poolside Bar and grilled fare
Swizzle Lounge – Bar. Cocktails priced at $9 to $11. Other drinks from $6.
Starbucks – Quick service location.

There are however a few downsides to this resort: guests staying at Cabana Bay will NOT receive complimentary Express Passes - this is usually cited as one of the main reasons for staying on site. Guests will also not be able to reach the hotel via water taxis and must use buses instead or be prepared to walk up to 25 minutes from their room to the theme parks and *CityWalk*. Parking is charged at $10 per night for self-parking, payable at check-in.

Chapter 4
Getting there:

Before we get too carried away with all the fun you can have at the Universal Orlando, you must first make your way there. Here are some of your options:

By car:

Universal Orlando is located about 10 miles southwest of the city of Orlando, Florida and about 10 miles northeast of the Walt Disney World resort. Universal can be reached easily by car from the Interstate 4 (I-4) and then following Universal Blvd north to the parking garages. For your GPS, the address you want is 6000 Universal Blvd, Orlando.

The parking garages are very big and can accommodate about 20,000 vehicles so be sure to remember where you parked. Garages open at least 90 minutes before official park opening time and all levels except the roof level are covered which means you will not come back to a car that has been in the sunlight all day or have to walk through the rain to get to your vehicle.

There is an easy to remember parking system - each parking spot is assigned a character name and a number - make sure to note it down as it could save you hours later on! A good tip is to take a photo of your parking location (but also write it down in case your phone or camera battery dies). The garages are located approximately 5 to 10 minutes walk away from the theme parks.

Parking is charged at $17 a day for self-parking (free for Preferred and Premium Annual Passholders). Preferred parking is $22 (discounted for Preferred Annual Passholders and free for Premier Passholders) and valet parking is $30 a day ($15 for Preferred Annual Passholders and free for Premier Passholders). "Red carpet valet" parking is available for a surcharge that guarantees you will get your car within 5 minutes.

Disabled parking bays are available; just make sure to request them. These are located slightly closer to CityWalk and the theme parks.

Lunchtime visitors to CityWalk can get free valet parking by asking for their restaurant receipt to be validated from Monday to Friday for two hours of free arking. Contact your restaurant for the specific hours of this offer. A signposted passenger drop-off point is also available.

If you are only coming to the resort for the evening, between 6:00pm and 10:00pm it is $5 to park for visitors, and parking is free for Florida residents with proof of residency. After 10:00pm parking is free for all guests – a good reason to visit CityWalk in the evening. However, for busy evenings like Halloween Horror Nights expect parking to be full price throughout the entire day.

After parking you will walk to the main parking rotunda hub, go through bag check and then walk through CityWalk – at the end of CityWalk you can turn left for *Islands of Adventure* or right for *Universal Studios Florida*.

Walt Disney World to Universal Orlando by car:
This is a common route as many visitors to Universal Orlando start off their vacation at the Walt Disney World resort. The Walt Disney World resort is large but you will first have to follow internal resort signs to the Interstate 4 (I-4). There are entrances to the I4 by ESPN: Wide World of Sports, Disney's Pop Century Resort, Disney's Typhoon Lagoon water park, and Downtown Disney/Disney Springs.

Follow the I-4 North/East and follow the road for 6 to 8 miles depending on where you got on, take exit 75A and merge onto Universal Blvd, the address you want is "6000 Universal Blvd, Orlando" but at this point you will be able to follow local road signs to the parking garages.

Public Transport:

There are two options for those using public transport - the I-Ride Trolley and the Lynx buses. The I-Ride follows a route along International Drive and is aimed at tourists only, whereas Lynx buses are used frequently by locals and are often busier at peak times.

Both services have a stop just outside Wet n' Wild water park which is where you should get off (on the I-Ride this is stop 8). From there it is a 15 to 20 minute walk. Cross the road and head north on Universal Blvd towards the theme parks until you reach the overhead walkway, which you will use to enter Universal Orlando.

Both options are fairly inexpensive at about $2 each - we recommend you look at both options online and decide on which is best for you.

Note: Be careful! You do have to cross a few major roads and one smaller road (which does not have traffic lights) on the short walk from the bus stops to the Universal Orlando resort. This walk should not take longer than 10 to 15 minutes.

Top Tip: Orlando public transport can be very infrequent with sometimes only 1 or 2 buses an hour so be sure to check the schedule in advance.

Walt Disney World to Universal Orlando by public transport:

This is a common route as many visitors to Universal Orlando start off their vacation at the Walt Disney World resort. Get to the Transportation and Ticket Center (TTC) on Walt Disney World resort property, for most guests this will involve getting to Magic Kingdom Park and then taking the monorail over to the TTC. At the TTC ask a Cast Member for the location of the LYNX bus stop. Alternatively you can catch the bus at Downtown Disney – we recommend you use Google Maps to locate this top. At either the TTC or Downtown Disney, you will catch the number 50 LYNX bus.

Be sure to have exact change for the bus as there is no change from the fare machine – the machine accepts coins and dollar bills. Make sure to ask the bus driver for a transfer (valid for 90 minutes from first issue) as you will be using more than one bus and this way you will only need to pay once. At the time of writing, the price is $2 per person.

Once you are on the number 50 bus you will be on it for approximately 35 minutes until you reach the first stop on Sea Harbor Drive. The exact location of the stop you will want to get off at is "6800 Sea Harbor Dr and Central Florida Pky".

Here you will need to wait for the number 8 LYNX bus and stay on that bus until "6200 International Dr and Universal Blvd". Be sure to ask the driver for the Universal stop if you are unsure. This number 8 bus journey will take about 15 minutes.

From here you will walk to Universal Orlando resort – the journey will take about 10 minutes. The total journey time with transfers is about 1 hour 15 minutes to 1 hour 30 minutes each way.

Take a look at http://www.golynx.com/ for help with the LYNX bus serve, including instructional videos and maps.

Shuttles from Orlando International Airport:

Unlike guests staying at Walt Disney World's on-site hotels there is no complimentary shuttle or motor coach transportation between the Universal Orlando resort and Orlando International Airport.

Many companies provide a shuttle service. We have found Mears Transportation to be reliable, though many other services are available. Super Shuttle also seems reliable. Prices are about between $30 to $35 per person return, or $20 one way.

Walt Disney World to Universal Orlando by shuttle:
A SuperShuttle charter quote for this route is about $45 for a 4-seater vehicle for a one-way trip, excluding tip. A taxi will work out cheaper. See below.

Taxi from the Orlando International Airport:

This is the option we recommend if you coming from the airport and do not want to drive - especially if there are several of you. The cost should not usually be more than about $55-70 including a tip each way. Mears Transportation also offer a taxi service and we have found them to be reliable, though many other services are available.

Walt Disney World to Universal Orlando by taxi:
Taxi prices vary but a quote (from Mears for example) will usually be about $35 for a taxi from Epcot to Universal Orlando, excluding tip. UberX quotes vary from $20 to $35.

Chapter 5

Universal Studios Florida - Park Guide

Universal Studios Florida opened in 1990 as the Floridian cousin to the popular Universal Studios theme park in Hollywood. The original idea of the park was to experience how movies are made and for actual movies to be made in the park too. Over the years the focus of the park has changed slightly and the philosophy is now to ride and "experience the movies" for yourself, as well as learn a bit about movie making in the process. The park hosted 7.06 million guests in 2013.

Note: Average attraction waits noted in this section here are estimates for busy summer days when on school break. Wait times may well be lower at other times of the year - they may also occasionally be higher, especially during the week of 4th July and around Christmas and New Year. When we list restaurant food prices, this information was accurate during our last visit to the restaurant - it may have since changed. We also do not post the full menu but just a sample of the food on offer. Meal prices stated in this section do not include a drink unless otherwise stated. When an attraction is listed as requiring lockers, all lose items must be stored in complimentary lockers outside each attraction.

Production Central

Production Central is the gateway to Universal Studios Florida - you must pass through it to get to the rest of the park and you will walk through it again when exiting. As far as attractions are concerned, here you will find **Despicable Me: Minion Mayhem, Hollywood Rip Ride Rockit, Shrek 4D** and **TRANSFORMERS: The Ride-3D**.

Production Central is also where **Guest Services** is located where you can get assistance with any guest issues including disability assistance, dining reservations, questions, compliments and complaints. You can also exchange some currencies at this location. Guest Services is located to the right-hand side after the turnstiles. To the left of the turnstiles you will find lockers, as well as stroller and wheelchair rentals.

The **Studio Audience Center** (to the right after the turnstiles) is the place to get tickets for any shows being filmed in the soundstages at the Universal Orlando resort. Tickets are complimentary. This is also the location for Lost and Found.

First Aid is located next to the Studio Audience Center. Another First Aid station is located between Louie's Italian Restaurant and Beetlejuice's Graveyard Revenue.

You will also find the **American Express Passholder Lounge** in this area of the park, opposite the Shrek attraction shop. This lounge is reserved for those who use an AmEx card to buy park tickets or an annual pass. Inside the lounge you will find bottled water, snacks and phone charging facilities. Simply show your ticket receipt and ticket itself, as well as your AmEx card for entry. Guests who simply use an AmEx card for in-park purchases but have not used it to purchase their entry tickets into the park do not have access to this lounge.

If you need to **mail** something, you can drop off your letters and postcards at the mailbox, located to the left as you come in after the turnstiles, to the right of the lockers. Stamps can be bought from the *On Location* shop here on the Front Lot. **Calling cards** can be bought from a vending machine near the lockers.

Family & Health Services, which includes a nursing room, is located to the right after the turnstiles.

Despicable Me: Minion Mayhem

Park area: Production Central
Height Restriction: 40 inches (1.02m)
Attraction length: 4 minutes + 2 pre-shows totaling 12 minutes
Express Pass Available: Yes
Average Wait: 60-120 minutes
Lockers required: No

A simulator based ride with several individual simulator vehicles in front of one screen featuring 4D effects. The ride itself we feel is quite rough with limited actions and a lot of "bumping" into other characters. In total the pre-show seemed to outdo the actual attraction itself but 'Despicable Me' fans will come out very excited nonetheless. Due to the low hourly capacity and the immense popularity of its characters, queues are almost always lengthy for this attraction.

Fun fact: The trees planted outside the ride are banana trees, as the minions love the yellow fruit so much!

Hollywood Rip Ride Rockit

Park area: Production Central
Height Restriction: Minimum 51 inches (1.29m) / Maximum 79 inches (2.00m)
Capacity: 1850 people per hour
Attraction length: 1 minute 45 seconds
Express Pass Available: Yes
Average Wait: 45-90 minutes
Lockers required: Yes

One of the newer experiences in the park, this coaster (the tallest in Orlando) truly dominates the skyline of the park. Once you board the vehicle get ready to be held in by just a lap bar-style restraint. Pull it down and now it is time to choose a song. As you ride you will get to hear your song pump into your ears as your adrenaline races. Think *Rock n Rollercoaster* at Disney but with more choices, without the loops and a huge drop. The initial almost-a-loop is really fun, as you stay upright all the way round - a really unique experience. One you are done you can even purchase an on-ride music video of your entire experience - awesome! A single rider line is available.

Top Tip: Don't trust the single rider wait time that is posted at the entrance to the attraction. The wait time from the bottom of the stairs to being on the train is usually approximately 30 minutes so walk in to the line and determine the time yourself from that. We have often waited less than half of the official posted single rider wait.

Top Tip 2: There are many secret bonus songs to choose from, as well as the ones shown to you. After lowering your restraint you will need to push and hold the ride logo for about 10 seconds and then type in a three-digit number. A full list of the songs is available online with a quick search.

Top Tip 3: The Pocket RockIt Rollercoaster Setlist iPhone app, available on the Apple App Store, lists the full song list including hidden songs. The app costs $0.99.

Shrek 4-D

Park area: Production Central
Height Restriction: None
Capacity: 2500-3000 people per hour
Attraction length: 12 minutes main show + 5 minutes pre-show
Express Pass Available: Yes
Average Wait: 15 to 45 minutes
Lockers required: No

Stepping into Shrek 4D, you know you are getting into a different kind of attraction – even Universal acknowledges that is not merely a 3D, but a 4D experience. The unique feature of this attraction is the seats which are able to create incredible sensations, acting like personal simulators. For those not wishing to experience the seat movement, a limited number of stationary seats are also available. The film itself is interesting and is great fun both for fans and non-fans of Shrek alike with some corny jokes and jabs at Disney thrown in for good measure.

TRANSFORMERS: The Ride-3D

Park area: Production Central
Height Restriction: 40 inches (1.02m)
Capacity: Approximately 1800 people per hour
Attraction length: 4 minutes 30 seconds
Express Pass Available: Yes
Average Wait: 90 to 150 minutes.
Lockers required: No

TRANSFORMERS is a 3D screen-based moving ride, similar to *The Amazing Adventures of Spiderman* in *Universal's Islands of Adventure*. For those who have never watched Transformers, the storyline follows Autobots trying to get the AllSpark. The ride is an enjoyable experience but in our opinion it just does not live up to how good a ride *Spiderman* is - considering *Spiderman* is a 15 year old ride it feels like almost no technological or storytelling progress has been made since then comparing the two. This ride will often have the longest queues in the park, after the rides in *The Wizarding World of Harry Potter: Diagon Alley*. A single rider line is available.

Fun fact: Ever wondered how such a long ride is packed into such a small building? The ride engineering came up with an ingenious way of reduce the ride's overall footprint as Universal Orlando is very much constrained by space: during the ride whilst you are watching a scene on one of the giant screens you are actually taken in an elevator up one floor which houses another level of ride track. Here the ride continues its course and towards the end of the ride you come back down to the first floor via another elevator whilst your focus is on another giant screen – this is all done seamlessly and really is an admirable technological feat.

Restaurants:
Universal Studios' Classic Monster Cafe - Quick Service. Accepts Universal Dining Plan. Serves chicken, lasagna, cheeseburgers, pizza and more. Entrees are priced at $7.50 to $11.50.

New York:

TWISTER...Ride it Out

Park area: New York
Height Restriction: None
Attraction length: 12 minutes
Express Pass Available: Yes
Average Wait: Less than 15 minutes
Lockers required: No

Ever wondered what it is like to experience a real tornado? Find out by feeling a simulated one for yourself in a controlled environment. This attraction is frightening due to its intensity and how loud it is so young children should avoid it. You may also get wet.

Editor's note: We do not expect this attraction to stick around for much longer and would not be surprised to see it demolished and replaced by a new offering over the coming years.

Fun fact: Look out for a reference to a Ghostbusters show that used to be in the park. You can find the reference in the ride's queue line - in one of the firehouse windows look closely and you'll see an ad for the Paranormal Travel Agency.

Revenge of the Mummy

Park area: New York
Height Restriction: 48 inches (1.22m)
Capacity: 2000 people per hour
Attraction length: 4 minutes
Express Pass Available: Yes
Average Wait: 20 to 60 minutes
Lockers required: Yes

A incredibly unique rollercoaster featuring fire, smoke, forward motion, backwards motion, turns and much more. The whole ride is fantastic starting off as a dark ride and developing into a coaster and is a definite must-do. Although the ride does not go upside down and is not exactly the fastest attraction in Orlando, it does tell its story very well and really immerses you in the atmosphere. It is a great thrill with plot twists throughout. A single rider line is available.

The queue line is also really good and contains several interactive elements. For example, there is a scarab beetle that you can press in the queue line whilst watching other guests via a screen. If you press the beetle, the on-screen guests will feel a quick blast of air from underneath them, guaranteed to give them a fright. But beware where you put your hands in line, as the treasure you see around you may not be all you think it is and you might just be in for a surprise or two.

Fun fact: The Mummy ride replaced Kongfrontation (a ride based on King Kong), which was once housed in the same building so a statue of the great ape has been left behind as a tribute in the treasure room.

The Blues Brothers Show
Get ready to see Jake and Elwood, the Blues Brothers themselves, take to the stage in this non-traditional show. Unlike other shows where you have to arrive in good time and sit in a show-style amphitheater, the Blues Brothers Show is simply on a small stall in a street in the New York area of the park. This show is a little bit lower key than others and has more of a street-mosphere feel to it. You can turn up just before the show starts and get a perfect view so there is no need to plan to see this one. Crowds are not very big and most people just walk in and out during the show. This is not one of our favorite shows in the park to be perfectly honest.

Restaurants:
Finnegan's Bar and Grill - Table Service location. Accepts Universal Dining Plan. Serves salads, sandwiches, fish and chips, chicken, corned beef, sirloin steak and more. Entrees are priced at $10 to $22. Our favorite places to eat in this park outside of Diagon Alley.

Louie's Italian Restaurant - Quick Service location. Accepts Universal Dining Plan. Serves spaghetti and meatballs, pizza slices, whole pizza pies and fettuccine alfredo. Entrees priced at $6 to $14. Whole pizza pies priced between $29 and $36.

San Francisco

Beetlejuice's Graveyard Revue

Park area: San Francisco
Height Restriction: None
Show length: 24 minutes
Express Pass Available: Yes
Lockers required: No

The Beetlejuice Graveyard Revue is a fun show filled with high-tempo music, classic monsters, and some decent live singing and dancing. However, the show is beginning to show its age, even after being updated in early 2014. The music in the show is mostly from decades past and we are surprised the show is even still in production. Surprisingly, there is very little screen time given to Beetlejuice himself. Go into the show with low expectations and you will probably enjoy it - go in expecting something mind-blowing and you might just leave disappointed.

Disaster!

Park area: San Francisco.
Height Restriction: None
Attraction length: 20 minutes
Express Pass Available: Yes
Average Wait: 20 to 60 minutes
Lockers required: No

This is your chance to become part of the cast of a motion picture that is being filmed right inside *Universal Studios Florida*. Guess what? They need actors to star in a disaster movie and who could be better than you? The first room is where guests volunteer to be part of the movie - they need everyone from a strong man to a grandma, so everyone is able to participate. This initial bit is fairly funny and there always seem to be people willing to get involved. Once the actors have been decided you move into the filming location where each of the actors performs a stunt. Then it is time for the ride portion of the attraction where you all get to become actors as you board a subway train in New York and things go very, very wrong...

Restaurants:
Richter's Burger Co. - Quick Service location. Accepts Universal Dining Plan. Serves cheeseburgers, salads, and chicken sandwiches. Entrees priced $8 to $10.50.
Lombard's Seafood Grille - Table Service location. Accepts Universal Dining Plan. Serves salads, sandwiches, catch of the day, sirloin steak, stir-fry and more. Entrees priced $9 to $20.

San Francisco Pastry Company - Sandwiches and Pastries location. Accepts Universal Dining Plan. Entrees priced $3 to $9.50.

World Expo

MEN IN BLACK: Alien Attack

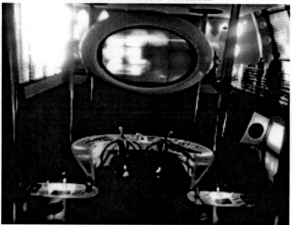

Park area: World Expo.
Height Restriction: 42 inches (1.07m)
Capacity: 2200 people per hour
Attraction length: 5 minutes
Express Pass Available: Yes
Average Wait: Less than 45 minutes
Lockers required: Yes

Shooting-type rides can often become annoying and repetitive but here at Men In Black it is your turn to defeat the aliens and protect the city. You are dispatched in teams and not only do you compete to destroy aliens, you are battling against another car - shoot that car and you will send it spinning. This ride is a great, fun, immersive experience that we highly recommend and makes for a great family attraction (subject to the height restriction). A single rider line is available.

Top Tip: Keep holding down the trigger throughout the ride. You get points for just doing this regardless of whether you hit any targets or not. For major points you will need to find and shoot Frank the Pug who is hidden in the ride. You will find Frank in the newspaper stand on the right hand side of the second room.

The Simpsons Ride

Park area: World Expo
Height Restriction: 40 inches (1.02m)
Capacity: 1600 people per hour
Attraction length: 6 minutes
Express Pass Available: Yes
Average Wait: 20 to 40 minutes.
Lockers required: No. Bags are stowed on the ground to the side of the simulator car.

How about riding a simulated rollercoaster? If that sounds like something you would be interested then the Simpsons characters have you covered. This is a fun filled simulator in front of a giant screen. Your adventure is filled with gags throughout and overall is a fun family experience. What's more the ride is surprisingly long and you are sure to be come out laughing.

Fun fact: During the pre-show video keep an eye out for the DeLorean car and Doc Brown from Back to the Future. Simpsons replaced the Back to the Future ride that utilized the same building and this is Universal's tribute.

Fear Factor Live

Park area: World Expo
Height Restriction: None
Capacity: 1800 people per show
Show length: 20 minutes
Express Pass Available: Yes
Lockers required: No

Get ready to watch real theme park guests compete against each other in Fear Factor Live, as they face their fears live on stage. Or alternatively why not apply and be one of those guests? If you would like to participate in the show you will want to be near the entrance 60 to 90 minutes before the next show is scheduled to start. Guests must be over 18, have photo ID on them and be in good physical condition to participate. Volunteers are also chosen to play minor roles during the show.

Restaurants:
Fast Food Boulevard - Quick Service location. Accepts Universal Dining Plan. From the outside this location appears to be several separate Simpson's-themed buildings. Inside you will find one big ordering area. You will find:

- **Moe's Tavern** sells Buzz Cola, Flaming Moes and Duff Beer (priced $3 to $8)
- **Lisa's Teahouse of Horror** sells salads and wraps (priced $6 to $10)
- **Luigi's** which sells personal-sized pizzas (priced $7 to $8)
- **The Frying Dutchman** sells fish (priced $4 to $14)
- **Cletus' Chicken Shack** sells fried chicken and chicken sandwiches (priced $8 to $11)
- **Krusty Burger** sells burgers and hot dogs ($8 to $13),

Hollywood:

Universal's Horror Make Up Show

Park area: Hollywood
Height Restriction: None
Show length: Approximately 25 minutes
Express Pass Available: Yes
Lockers required: No

A fun show that is sure to have you in stitches. The Horror Make Up show is a great chance to see behind the scenes at how gory and scary effects are accomplished in films. The show's script is very well thought out with laugh after laugh and there is some fun audience interaction too. This is one show we highly recommend you visit! The theatre is relatively small so make sure to arrive early.

If you want to be selected to be part of the show, the actors tend to go for young women located in the middle section of the theatre.

Note: The show has set performance times and usually runs about every 45 minutes.

Terminator 2: 3-D

Park area: Hollywood
Height Restriction: None
Capacity: 2500 to 2800 people per hour
Show length: About 25 minutes total including the main show (12 minutes) + pre-show
Express Pass Available: Yes
Average Wait: Less than 25 minutes

Terminator 2: 3-D incredible mix of live-action, 3D and in-theatre special effects. This show is unlike any theme park show you have ever seen and is hugely enjoyable. The 3D is incredible well realized and merges extremely well with the live actors, meaning sometimes it is difficult to figure out what is on screen and what is actually in front of you.

A warning for those easily startled that there are some loud pyrotechnic bangs throughout the show and there are sudden jolts in the seats. There are stationary seats available. If you do not enjoy loud shows then Terminator 2 is most definitely not for you but it would be a shame to miss out on such an incredible show. The show runs at set times - usually about every 20 minutes.

Top Tip: There is usually no need to turn up more than 5 minutes before the posted time, as there are plenty of seats in the theatre for each show.

Lucy - A Tribute

Park area: Hollywood
Height Restriction: None
Attraction length: Walk-through
Express Pass Available: No
Average Wait: None. Walk-in exhibition.

A walk-through area featuring memorabilia from the life of Lucille Ball. You will see costumes, film scripts and you can even test your knowledge about the famous redhead with an interactive videogame.

Restaurants:
Mel's Drive In - Quick Service location. Serves cheeseburgers and root beer floats. Accepts Universal Dining Plan. Entrees priced $8 to $10.50.

Beverly Hills Boulangerie - Quick Service location. Accepts Universal Dining Plan. Serves sandwiches, pastries, cakes, soups and salads. Entrees priced $7 to $12.

Woody Woodpecker's Kid Zone

Important note: When the park is not very busy this area will open one hour after the regular park opening time.

Rumors say that this area of the park does not have very long left and the entire area could be disappearing in the near future with the exception of *E. T. Adventure*.

Animal Actors on Location

Park area: Woody Woodpecker's KidZone
Height Restriction: None
Show length: 20 minutes
Express Pass Available: Yes
Lockers required: No

A behind the scenes look at how animals are taught to act in films – there is even some audience participation. In our opinion, the show is lackluster with a big reliance on clips and a lack of flow – kids will love the show though. It is a shame to see this show not being hugely entertaining, especially when compared to a similar show at Walt Disney World's Animal Kingdom that only features birds – Disney's show one has humor, a great storyline and a real wow factor. This one just doesn't. We would advise you to give this a miss unless you are a big animal fan.

A Day in the Park with Barney

Park area: Woody Woodpecker's KidZone
Height Restriction: None
Show length: 15 minutes
Express Pass Available: Yes
Lockers required: No

Come and join Barney and his friends for a fun-filled show where little ones can sing along to some of their favorite songs. After the show is over, this is a play area too to explore, and before or after the main show you can usually meet and have a photo taken with Barney.

Curious George Goes to Town

A play area filled with water so be sure to bring a change of clothes for the little ones.

Top Tip: If you want to walk through the area and go to the factory without getting wet, simply follow the signposted "dry path".

Woody Woodpecker's Nuthouse Coaster

Park area: Woody Woodpecker's KidZone
Height Restriction: 36 inches (0.92m)
Capacity: 780 people per hour
Attraction length: 44 seconds
Express Pass Available: Yes
Average Wait: 30 minutes or less
Lockers required: No

Think of *Woody Woodpecker's Nuthouse Coaster* as a kid's first coaster - a way to get them introduced into the world of coasters before trying something a bit more intense. The ride is great fun for the little ones or just for those not wanting to jump on the likes of *The Hulk* just yet.

Fievel's Playland
A play area for the little ones to let off some steam. There is quite a bit of water to play with and in the hot Floridian sun it is sure that your kids will want to get stuck in – so be sure to bring a change of clothes. There is even a small water slide in this area with dinghies.

E.T. Adventure

Park area: Woody Woodpecker's KidZone
Height Restriction: 34 inches (0.87m)
Attraction length: 4 minutes 30 seconds
Express Pass Available: Yes
Average Wait: 20 minutes or less
Lockers required: No

A cute, if ageing, ride where you sit on bicycles like in the E.T. movie and soar through the sky whilst trying to keep E.T. safe. It is a fun little ride with a fairly high capacity and one of the few Universal Studios Florida classics. The ride system is very similar to *Peter Pan's Flight* in Disney's *Magic Kingdom* and it makes for a truly immersive experience.

Restaurants:
There are no restaurants in the "Woody Woodpecker's Kidzone" area of the park.

The Wizarding World of Harry Potter – Diagon Alley

This expansion of the Wizarding World made its public debut in July 2014; a larger and even more detailed area of the Wizarding World, even surpassing the level of authenticity of the original Hogsmeade land in Islands of Adventure.

Diagon Alley is not seen by Muggles – non-Wizards – so the whole of this area of the park is hidden behind a huge façade of London's Waterfront. On the waterfront you will find facades of several famous London landmarks.

Here is a glimpse of what this embankment area looks like:

You will find facades here of: King's Cross Station, Foyles bookstore on Charing Cross Road, Leicester Square tube station, Wyndham's Theatre and 12 Grimmauld Place – home of the Black family in the books and films.

Hidden secret: One cool feature of the waterfront is on the Grimmauld Place building. If you look carefully at the windows every once in a while the curtain of one of them will open and Kreature, the house elf from the Harry Potter series, will peer outside at the muggles.

As well as the detailed facades, in front of Wyndham's Theatre visitors see the Statue of Eros (which in real London is actually located in Piccadilly Circus, but we will allow this incongruity for some theme park magic) and the only sign that this is a Harry Potter entry area – the Purple Knight Bus. This Knight Bus features an interactive shrunken head experience as seen in the Prisoner of Azkaban film – more on this later in this section, as well as a meet and greet with the conductor.

Visitors enter Diagon Alley through the façade of Leicester Square tube station and transition into the Wizarding World and Diagon Alley by a series of walls with strange brick shapes and sound effects.

Once inside, Diagon Alley is laid out before you with shops on both sides, and the iconic Gringotts Bank at the end of the road. Gringotts Bank houses the premiere attraction of Diagon Alley, which we will come to later in the guide. It even features a fire-breathing dragon on the roof.

Shops:
There are an incredible variety of shops in the main stretch of Diagon Alley.
- **Quality Quidditch Supplies (shop)** – This shop will carry all kinds of Quidditch themed merchandise, including apparel, hats and pendants, as well as brooms, Golden Snitches, Bludgers and bats and Quaffles.
- **Weasleys' Wizard Weezes (shop)** – This three-story shop features all kinds of prank-filled items and toys, as well as novelty items and magic tricks. A sample of what will be on offer includes: Extendable Ears, Decoy Detonators and Fangled Flyers.
- **Madam Malkin's (shop)** – Guests will find all variety of wizard themed clothing here. Including complete Hogwarts school uniforms, with ties, robes, scarves, and more on offer. Other apparel and jewelry themed to the four school houses will also be available.
- **Ollivander's (experience/ short show and shop)** – This experience is very similar to that of Ollivander's in Hogsmeade. The difference is that there are several rooms

performing shows simultaneously. Guests will also be able to purchase a unique Ollivander's wand, or choose from a variety of character replica wands.

- **Wiseacre's Wizarding Equipment (shop)** – Find all kinds of wizardry essentials here. From hourglasses to compasses, and telescopes to binoculars. Plus themed apparel.
- **Wands by Gregorovitch (shop)** – Come purchase your wands from this legendary wandmaker's shop.
- **Shutterbuttons (shop)** – Get a personalized video of you in the wizarding world. Stand in front of a green screen and perform various actions in 12 exciting locations then you will get a "moving picture" made for you just like the newspapers in Harry Potter. At launch these moving pictures are being provided on DVD in a collectors tin, with a moving photo frame option coming in the future, as well as an MP4 video option. Pricing is currently $49.95. Up to 4 people can partake in the experience together. You will be supplied with Potter robes to fit right in but you must bring your own wand if you want one in the video.

Restaurants:
Fans of the young boy wizard will definitely not go hungry in Diagon Alley due to the wealth of dining options available:

- **Leaky Cauldron (restaurant)** – Quick service location. Accepts Universal Dining Plan, but not quick service. This location serves tradition English fare such as Banger's and Mash, cottage Pie, Toad in the Hole, Fish and Chips and much more. Entrees priced at $9 to $20.
- **Florean Fortescue's Ice Cream (restaurant)** – Quick service location. Serves themed ice cream and other cold treats. Does not accept the Universal Dining Plan. Ice cream flavors include: Granny Smith, Earl Grey and Lavender, Clotted Cream, Orange Marmalade, and Butterbeer flavor just to name a few. This location also serves breakfast items and pastries in the morning. Ice creams priced at $5 to $13.

As well as the above locations which guests can explore, there are a number of shop fronts which guests cannot step inside of. Nevertheless, these will undoubtedly make for great photo opportunities. Expect to see the offices of the Daily Prophet, Broomstix, Flourish and Blotts and many others.

Knockturn Alley:

Running alongside Diagon Alley, is the darker "Knockturn Alley", described as a "gloomy back street" by Universal. The shops and storefronts here are filled with items related to Dark Magic. The flagship store in this area is **Borgin and Burkes**, which sells dark items such as Death Eater masks, skulls and other sinister objects – plus make sure to check out the vanishing cabinet.

This area is covered so as to look continually dark and give a nighttime atmosphere, so expect it to be popular when one of Orlando's frequent rain showers makes its appearance. Be sure to look out for the animated "Wanted" posters of the Death Eaters. There are many interactive wand experiences available in this area of the land (more on these later).

There are also two other streets to explore in Diagon Alley with themed shop fronts and interactive wand touches – Horizont Alley and Carkitt Market.

Attractions:
Harry Potter and the Escape from Gringotts

Height Restriction: 42 inches (1.07m)
Attraction length: 5 minutes
Express Pass Available: No
Lockers required: Yes
Average Waits: 90 to 250 minutes

Outside the bank, marvel at the fire breathing dragon on the roof.
Then, once inside the bank, you prepare for the experience of a
lifetime. The queue line begins by going past several iconic
locations: you will see the animatronic Goblins hard at work in the
grand marble lobby, as well as wizard vaults and go through a
security area (where you have your photo taken). Just like the 'Harry
Potter and the Forbidden Journey' ride in Islands of Adventure, this
attraction's queue line is as much of an experience as the ride itself.
The storyline begins to unfold as you see signs of Harry, Ron and
Hermione discussing their plans.

The ride itself is a rollercoaster-type attraction which is described as "multidimensional" by Universal and mixes a variety of real world elements with footage on screens, much like 'Forbidden Journey'. Although there are drops and turns (but no loops or inversions) in the layout, think of this more as a 3D-experience ride than a rollercoaster – it is more *Transformers* than *The Incredible Hulk*, but at the same time completely unlike both of these. The ride features 4K-high definition technology as well as 3D screens, with glasses being worn by riders.

Spoiler alert: The ride is inspired by the final film "Harry Potter and the Deathly Hallows – Part 2," and a pivotal scene where Harry, Ron and Hermione break into Gringotts bank to steal a powerful Horcrux that will help them defeat Lord Voldemort. On Harry Potter and the Escape from Gringotts, you will encounter the trio during this quest – but expect to meet some dangerous creatures and malicious villains as well! During the ride you will come face to face with Bellatrix Lestrange, security trolls, fire breathing dragons and even Voldemort himself.

A single rider line is available, but it skips all indoor scenes and leads directly to the loading area. Remember that the queue line scenes are a significant part of the experience here but if all you want is the ride itself, the single rider line can save you a huge amount of time.

Kings Cross Station and the Hogwarts Express:

Height Restriction: None

Attraction length: About 5 minutes in each direction.
Express Pass Available: No
Lockers required: No
Average Waits: 15 to 60 minutes (A park-to-park ticket is required)

The final area and attraction to explore in the Diagon Alley expansion is Kings Cross Station. Guests can enter Kings Cross Station and admire it in all its beauty – faithfully recreated – and then break through the platform's wall and arrive on platform 9 ¾ where you will be able to catch the Hogwarts Express, which will transport you through the countryside to Hogsmeade Station (located at Universal's Islands of Adventure park). The journey lasts several minutes and as you look out of the windows of the train you will see stories unfold – all on a real full-sized train, with compartments to sit in just like Harry and his friends did in the films.

During the journey you can gaze out of the windows and see Hagrid on his motorcycle, the English countryside, Buckbeak the Hippogriff, the purple Knightbus, the Weasley twins on brooms, and even Dementors. There are more surprises in store too. Each of the Hogwarts Express trains seats 200 passengers, with trips in each direction being unique.

Once you hop off the train at Hogsmeade you will be able to explore the area and the Harry Potter themed attractions including the incredible 'Harry Potter and the Forbidden Journey' ride. This train is the first ever inter-park ride!

Important: In order to experience the Hogwarts Express attraction visitors must have a park-to-park ticket. A single park ticket will not allow visitors to experience this ride – guests will still, of course, be able to experience each of the theme parks' Wizarding Worlds on separate days but not use the Hogwarts Express to travel between them.

Interactive Wand Experiences:

An interactive wand experience is available at the Wizarding World, both at Diagon Alley and Hogsmeade – this additional experience launched with the opening of Diagon Alley. In order to participate, guests must purchase an interactive wand from the Wizarding World priced at $45, around $10 more than the non-interactive wands.

Once you have purchased a wand, look for bronze medallions embedded in the streets that mark the various shop windows where you can cast spells. A map of the locations is included with each wand. Once you are standing on one of the medallions, just perform the correct spell (by drawing the shape of the spell in the air with your wand and saying the name of the spell – all shown on the medallions on the floor) and watch the magic come to life. This is a really fun bit of extra entertainment, especially as your wands can be reused again and again during future visits.

Diagon Alley Entertainment:
Diagon Alley features several pieces of live entertainment in the same way that Hogsmeade does in Islands of Adventure. Inside the Carkitt Market area, two shows are performed daily:

The first show brings to life two fables from **The Tales of Beedle the Bard** – "The Fountain of Fair Fortune" and "The Tale of the Three Brothers" (which was featured in the seventh film). Performed by a troupe of four from the Wizarding Academy of Dramatic Arts, this trunk show uses scenic pieces, props and puppetry fabricated by Emmy-award-winning designer Michael Curry.

The second show features a musical performance by **The Singing Sorceress: Celestina Warbeck and the Banshees**. With a whole lot of soul, this swinging show features never-before heard songs including "A Cauldron Full Of Hot, Strong Love," "You Stole My Cauldron But You Can't Have My Heart" and "You Charmed The Heart Right Out Of Me" – all titles created by J.K. Rowling. The lyrics also contain never-before-revealed information about Celestina's wand – written by J.K. Rowling for Pottermore.

As well as the live stage shows, the area features a host of other interactive experiences. Just outside Diagon Alley itself, by the London waterfront, you will find the **Knight Bus** and its two permanent occupants: a shrunken head and the Knight Bus Conductor, who will be more than happy to chat, joke around and take photos with you.

If you fancy owning some wizarding currency then be sure to stop by **Gringotts Money Exchange** where you are able to exchange your Muggle currency for Wizarding Bank Notes, which can be used within both Diagon Alley and Hogsmeade (as well as the rest of the two theme parks) to purchase snacks and items from the shops. The shops accept regular US dollars too but these Wizarding bank notes can make for a cool and cheap souvenir.

Universal Studios Florida Park Entertainment:

Universal's Superstar Parade

Expect to see the characters from Despicable Me - including Gru and the Minions, Sponge Bob Squarepants and Dora the Explorer, among other characters in the daily *Universal Superstar Parade*. This parade is great fun for those who are fans of characters. Both the floats and the characters are great to see as they dance along to music.

The parade route starts by the *Universal's Horror Make Up Show* attraction and moves across to the lagoon, past *TRANSFORMERS*, round the front of Revenge of the Mummy, down pasta the Universal Stage and Despicable Me and back along Hollywood Boulevard ending next to *Universal's Horror Make Up Show*.

One of the best things about *Universal's Superstar Parade* is that it is nowhere near as crowded as the nearby Disney park parades - many people simply do not know it exists; others just go to Universal for the thrills. Having said this, although the parade is enjoyable it is nowhere near the standards of a Disney parade and is very basic in its nature.

The parade is performed once each day - the time will be printed on your park map.

Top Tip: Twice per day, before the parade starts there are dance parties hosted by Mel's Drive-In twice. During the dance parties floats and characters from the parade will come out to meet and greet, dance and sign autographs.

Universal's Cinematic Spectacular - 100 Years of Movie Memories

Universal's way to bid you goodnight is with its nightly "Cinematic Spectacular", a nostalgic viewing of highlights from Universal movies of the last 100 years. The show takes place on the lagoon in the middle of the park and features water screens, a great soundtrack, fountains and fireworks. The show is thematically split up into categories such as humor and horror with clips from famous films shown on water curtains.

The 18-minute nighttime show will perhaps be more pertinent to adults than children due to the age of some of the clips - be aware that this is much more of a projection show than a fireworks show, with fireworks being few and far between.

If you do want a front row view then usually turning up even 30 minutes before the show's scheduled start time will guarantee you a place. If you do not fancy waiting that long then if you turn up only a few minutes before there should not be too many people in front of you as there is such a large viewing area.

Having said this, this is not a Disney or even SeaWorld-quality show in our opinion, and if you have high expectations you will be disappointed. Nevertheless, it is worth a viewing.

There is a dining experience option at Lombard's Seafood Grille available which gives you reserved seating for the show but even on peak summer days we never found the area around the lagoon to be crowded to the point where we would consider this option to be necessary. If you want to take part in this dining experience, reservations are required 24 hours in advance. Prices are $44.99 for adults and $12.99 for children and include an appetizer, entrée, dessert and one non-alcoholic beverage, as well as VIP viewing of the Spectacular. Make sure to confirm that it is taking place on the night you plan on dining there, as this offer is not necessarily available year-round.

There is a private viewing area in the Simpsons Fast Food Boulevard area that is reserved for VIP viewing of the cinematic spectacular in the evenings. Seating here is priced at $15 and is on offer 45 minutes before the show begins. The price of the VIP area includes one cupcake and one non-alcoholic beverages (excluding Flaming Moes) and gratuity too, meaning that the effective cost of the seating is about $8. If it is busy and you fancy a dessert this could be a good option for you.

2015 will be the 25th anniversary of the Universal Orlando resort and we expect the nighttime show to be either updated or completely redesigned. At the time of writing no official announcement has been made about this.

Chapter 6
Islands of Adventure - Park Guide:

Universal's Islands of Adventure opened in 1999 with many famed attractions instantly putting it on the world theme park map – we would argue even more so that *Universal Studios Florida* itself. The true revolution for the park, however, came with the opening of *The Wizarding World of Harry Potter*, and expansion and innovation has not stopped since. The park hosted 8.1 million guests in 2013 making it the more popular of the two Universal Orlando theme parks.

Port of Entry

Perhaps the most beautiful entrance to a theme park in America, *Port of Entry* transports you to a different time and place and shows that Universal really *does* think about its theming, despite what some lovers of other theme parks may say. There are no attractions in this area of the park but rather it acts as an entranceway to the islands of adventure themselves. You will find shops and few places to eat in this area.

To the right of the welcome arch at *Port of Entry* you will find **Guest Services** where you can get assistance with any guest issues including disability assistance, dining reservations, questions, compliments and complaints. **Lost and Found** is also located here.

Lockers, a **phone card vending machine** and a **payphone** are all located to the left of the archway. **Strollers** and **wheelchair rentals** can also be found here.

First Aid is located inside the Open Arms Hotel building to the right of the entrance archway. There is another first aid station in The Lost Continent area by the bazaar. Also on the right of the arch is guest services and lost and found.

Fun fact: At the wheelchair and stroller rental location look out for a sign which lists the pricing of rentals along with several hilarious items which have already been "rented out" including a gondola, an aero boat and a rocket car.

Restaurants:
Confisco Grill and Backwater Bar - Table service location. Accepts Universal Dining Plan. Serves wood-oven pizzas, sandwiches, pasta and fajitas. Entrees priced $9 to $18. The Backwater Bar has a happy hour that runs daily from 4:00pm to 7:00pm (subject to change).
Croissant Moon Bakery - Quick service location. Accepts Universal Dining Plan. Serves continental breakfasts, sandwiches, Paninis, cakes and branded coffee. Entrees are priced between $2.50 and $10. Note: This location is not listed on the map at all - it is on the right hand side of Port of Entry.

Starbucks – Quick service location. Does not accept the Universal dining plan. Located right next to Cinnabon.

Seuss Landing

Caro-Seuss-el

Park area: Seuss Landing
Height Restriction: None
Capacity: Approximately 1000 guests per hour
Attraction length: 2 minutes
Express Pass Available: Yes
Average Wait: Less than 15 minutes

This attraction is just like a normal carrousel type ride but themed to the Seuss series of books.

The Cat in the Hat

Park area: Seuss Landing
Height Restriction: 36 inches (0.92m) minimum to ride with an adult, or 48 inches (1.22m) to ride alone
Capacity: 1800 people per hour
Attraction length: 4 minutes
Express Pass Available: Yes
Average Wait: 15 to 45 minutes

A nice dark ride ride where you travel through the story of *The Cat in the Ha*t with your favorite characters, and spin along the way. Admittedly the ride makes much more sense if you have read the books or seen the films but anyone can appreciate this adventure.

Note: Guests under 36" may not ride. Guests 36" to 48" must ride with a supervising companion. Hand-held infants are not allowed.

If I Ran the Zoo
A play area for kids to run around, designed in a maze-like format. Good for big Dr Seuss fans with some in-jokes along the way. Unsurprisingly there is a water area too to cool down on the classic hot Floridian days.

One Fish, Two Fish, Red Fish, Blue Fish

Park area: Seuss Landing
Height Restriction: Children under 48 inches (1.22m) must ride with an adult
Capacity: 350 people per hour
Attraction length: 1 minute 30 seconds
Express Pass Available: Yes
Average Wait: 15 to 45 minutes

You have surely seen the classic spinning type rides before, like Dumbo in the Disney parks. But this ride packs a bit of a twist. You will want to follow along with what the famous Dr. Seuss song says in order to stay dry. So when you hear "up, up, up" you will want to steer yourself upwards and be as high as you can be to avoid getting soaked. This is a fun twist on what usually can be a bit of a repetitive, unimaginative ride. During colder times the water is turned off.

The High in the Sky Seuss Trolley Train Ride

Park area: Seuss Landing
Height Restriction: 40 inches (1.02m) minimum to ride (must be accompanied) or 48 inches (1.22m) to ride alone
Attraction length: 5 minutes
Express Pass Available: Yes
Average Wait: 15 to 45 minutes

A cute, slow journey across the rooftops in Seuss Landing. Note how there are no straight lines in this area as you go around the crazy land of Dr. Seuss.

Restaurants:
Circus McGurks Cafe Stoo-pendous - Quick Service location. Accepts Universal Dining Plan. Serves pizza, pasta, salads, cheeseburgers and chicken. Entrees priced at $7 to $9.

The Lost Continent

Poseidon's Fury

Park area: The Lost Continent
Height Restriction: None
Attraction length: 15 minutes
Express Pass Available: Yes
Average Wait: 15 to 45 minutes

This attraction is an interesting concept – it is a walk-through live show where your guide takes you deeper and deeper into the Temple of Poseidon. Some cool fire and water effects are used throughout the show but be prepared to stand for an extended period of time as you move from room to room throughout the show. The attraction does look much grander from the outside than it is on the inside. In our opinion it is not worth more than a 30-minute wait - it is a good attraction but if the queues are long we would recommend coming back later in the day.

The Eighth Voyage of Sindbad Stunt Show

Height Restriction: None
Show length: 22 minutes
Express Pass Available: Yes
Average Wait: None. Presented at scheduled times only.

This is an action-packed show with special effects at every opportunity. It is these effects, ironically, that are the main problem with the show for us: the show is just effect after effect without a decent storyline meaning the overall, the show can be described as "meh". If it is raining, this show is a good bit of shelter but otherwise we would recommend giving it a miss. In our opinion, this is the worst attraction in both parks. Note: To those who do not like loud bangs, avoid this show!

The Mystic Fountain
This is listed as an attraction on the map, but we would hesitate to really call it one. Essentially it a fountain that you can interact with and talk to. The fountain is usually very witty and it can be a good source of laughs. Beware though; the fountain loves to get people wet!

Restaurants:
Mythos Restaurant - Table Service location. Accepts Universal Dining Plan. Serves sandwiches, Shortribs, Asian Salmon and Mahi Mahi. Entrees priced $13 to $20. This is our favorite restaurant in the park. Note: Mythos is only open for lunch.

—

Fire Eater's Grill - Quick Service location. Accepts Universal Dining Plan. Serves hot dogs, chicken fingers, grilled gyro and salads. Entrees priced $8 to $9. Surprisingly large portions.

Fun fact: Behind Mythos Restaurant there is a bridge. Stand under it and you might just get to hear a troll!

The Wizarding World of Harry Potter - Hogsmeade

This was the addition to the park that truly put Universal Orlando on the world theme park map and made it a must-visit. Here you can step into the world of Harry Potter and experience what it is like to visit Hogsmeade - dine there, visit the shops and experience some wild rides. The area is incredibly well themed and Potter fans will be see authenticity unlike anywhere else. Throughout this guide you may see The Wizarding World of Harry Potter abbreviated to WWOHP.

To avoid any misconception we would like to clarify that this is just a land, albeit a very well themed one, and NOT an entire theme park as some of the press have reported in the past. It also existed several years before the Diagon Alley are opened over in the neighboring park.

Fun fact: In the restrooms at the Wizarding World, you can hear Moaning Myrtle, and in the rafters of Three Broomsticks you can see shadows of owls flying about.

Dragon Challenge

Park area: The Wizarding World of Harry Potter - Hogsmeade
Height Restriction: 54 inches (1.37m)
Capacity: 3500 people per hour
Attraction length: 2 minutes 25 seconds
Express Pass Available: Yes
Average Wait: 60 to 90 minutes

Re-themed from *Dueling Dragons* to its current incarnation for *The Wizarding World of Harry Potter: Hogsmeade*, the ride layout has remained the same. You will see Ron Weasley's car in the queue, enter Hogwarts and then fly on an incredible inverted coaster. There are actually two coasters here: the Hungarian Horntail or Chinese Fireball. You choose which track you will ride at the end of the line. If you want two different but equally fun experiences we recommend experiencing both.

Top Tip 1: During the first section of the Dragon Challenge queue there is a viewing area – here you can get some great photos of Hogwarts, perfectly framed. Alternatively it is a great place to watch the shows performed in this area of the park with no crowds.

Top Tip 2: Once you have experienced one of the rollercoasters, you can get in a shorter line for the second or re-ride the first. To do this, exit the ride as normal and when you leave the station building turn right where there is a gap in the railings and go up a path and some steps. Alternatively, if you simply wish to exit you can follow the regular path all the way to the exit and back to Hogsmeade.

Triwizard Spirit Rally

This show is a six-minute dance contest between two competing wizard schools: men versus women. The men's routine involves complex sword-fighting techniques, whilst the ladies dazzle with their ribbons and acrobatics. It is a nice bit of street/stage entertainment and a great photo opportunity. Though, do be prepared for a host with a terrible attempt at a British English accent.

Frog Choir

A nine-minute performance of Harry Potter film songs and magic-inspired music performed by Hogwarts students and their frogs - all done acapella with voices and no instruments, there is an almost beat-box flair to this show and it is a great piece of entertainment in what otherwise can be a very busy area of the park.

Flight of the Hippogriff

Park area: The Wizarding World of Harry Potter - Hogsmeade
Height Restriction: 36 inches (0.92m)
Capacity: 650 people per hour
Attraction length: 1 minute 5 seconds

Express Pass Available: Yes
Average Wait: 45 to 60 minutes

A small rollercoaster where you soar on a Hippogriff and go past Hagrid's hut. Good family fun and a good starter coaster before putting your children on the likes of *The Hulk*.

Harry Potter and the Forbidden Journey

Park area: The Wizarding World of Harry Potter - Hogsmeade
Height Restriction: 48 inches (1.22m)
Capacity: 2800 people per hour
Attraction length: 5 minutes
Express Pass Available: No
Average Wait: 45 to 90 minutes

A truly groundbreaking ride featuring projection screens, hugely flexible ride vehicles and an incredibly detailed queue. This was a turning point in Universal Orlando's history cementing its spot as one of the world's best theme park resorts. The ride vehicles move effortlessly from scene to scene, with incredible technology and a great, interesting storyline. The moment your enchanted bench first takes off is breathtaking. The queue line as well is almost an attraction in itself.

If you do not wish to experience the ride, you can still explore the inside of Hogwarts castle, simply ask one of the team members for the Tour Only entrance – this allows you to skip all of the locker line and bring cameras to take photos of the incredibly well themed interior.

This is a single rider line available too (more on Single Rider lines in Chapter 8). This can cut down wait times significantly; expected single rider waits are usually about 50-75% shorter than the standard wait time in our experience, though mileage may vary.

Hidden Secret: When you are in Dumbledore's office hearing his speech, take a look at the books on the wall to the right of him. Once in a while, one of the books may just do something very magical.

Hidden Secret 2: Look at the moving portraits of the four founders of Hogwarts; each of them is holding a Horcrux used to defeat Voldemort in the films and books.

Ollivander's

Park area: The Wizarding World of Harry Potter - Hogsmeade
Height Restriction: None
Capacity: 250 people per hour
Attraction length: 3 to 4 minutes
Express Pass Available: No
Average Wait: 30 to 60 minutes

Technically this is a pre-show to a shop. Get in line and you will go into Ollivander's in small groups of about 25 people. One person in the group will be chosen by the wizard to test out the right wand for them. Eventually the right one is found and they are given the opportunity to buy when the group is moved to Owl Post – the shop next door. This is a fantastic experience, which we highly recommend you visit. It is suitable for people of all ages.

Note: This is not listed as an attraction on the park map. There is no wait time sign at the front of the line either and the entrance to the line is not very clear - the entrance is the railings to the left-hand side of door to Ollivander's - a Team Member will be there to assist you if necessary. As mentioned in stats about the experience is about 4 minutes and it takes about 2 minutes to get people in and out. It is easy to estimate how long the queue is: do a quick headcount of the people in line in front of you - the wait is about 6 minutes for every 25 people ahead of you in the line.

Top Tip: An identical experience is also on offer at Ollivander's in *Diagon Alley* in Universal Studios Florida park next door, where the queue times are often shorter than at this location as there are three rooms running shows at the same time.

Hogsmeade Station and the Hogwarts Express:

Height Restriction: None
Attraction length: About 5 minutes in each direction.
Express Pass Available: No

Lockers required: No
Average Waits: 15 to 60 minutes (A park-to-park ticket is required)

The final area and attraction to explore in this area is Hogsmeade's station giving access to the Hogwarts Express. Guests can enter Hogsmeade Station and admire it in all its beauty and catch the Hogwarts Express, which will transport you through the countryside to Kings Cross Station (located at Universal Studios Florida park). The journey lasts several minutes and as you look out of the windows of the train you will see stories unfold – all on a real full-sized train, with compartments to sit in just like Harry and his friends did in the films.

During the journey you can gaze out of the windows and see Hagrid on his motorcycle, the English countryside, Buckbeak the Hippogriff, the purple Knightbus, the Weasley twins on brooms, and even Dementors. There are more surprises in store too. Each of the Hogwarts Express trains seats 200 passengers, with trips in each direction being unique.

Once you hop off the train at Kingds Cross you will be able to explore the area and the Harry Potter themed attractions there, including the innovative 'Harry Potter and the Escape from Gringotts' attraction! This train is the first ever inter-park ride!

Important: In order to experience the Hogwarts Express attraction visitors must have a park-to-park ticket. A single park ticket will not allow visitors to experience this ride – guests will still, of course, be able to experience each of the theme parks' Wizarding Worlds on separate days but not use the Hogwarts Express to travel between them.

Restaurants:

We highly recommend you take a look inside the Hog's Head and Three Broomsticks even if you do not plan to eat there to get the full Potter experience. Three Broomsticks in particular is an absolute masterpiece that should not be missed. Look upstairs in the rafters to see some cool details.

- **Hog's Head** - Quick Service location. Does not accept the Universal Dining Plan. This pub is located in the same building as the Three Broomsticks. Serves alcoholic beer, a selection of spirits, non-alcoholic Butterbeer and juices. Drinks $2.50 to $7.
- **Three Broomsticks -** Quick Service location. Accepts Universal Dining Plan. Serves breakfast meals inspired from around the world. At lunch and dinner you will find Cornish pasties, fish & chips, Shepard's pie, smoked turkey legs, rotisserie smoked chicken and spareribs. Entrees priced $8 to $15.

Drinks:
To maintain the integrity of the land, J.K. Rowling specified that no branded drinks be sold – so you will find no Coca Cola products here. You will only find Harry Potter branded drinks such as Butterbeer, water and some fruit squashes. You are of course from to buy any drink elsewhere in Islands of Adventure and bring it into the Wizarding World.

Shops:
The shops and merchandise in the Wizarding World are just as much an experience as some of the rides. Be sure to step inside and maybe you will even purchase a souvenir or two.

- **Filch's Emporium of Confiscated Goods** – This is the exit gift shop to the Harry Potter and the Forbidden Journey rides. Inside you will find everything from themed t-shirts to hats and scarves, and mugs to photo frames and trinkets. It has almost everything you could ever want. The shop also contains a few items themed to dark magic.
- **Honeydukes** – For those who have a sweet tooth, make sure to visit Honeydukes. You will find everything from love potion sweets to chocolate frogs (with include collectable

trading cards), and tons of other candy. For those who have visited *the Wizarding World* in the past, Zonko's Joke Shop is now gone and Honeydukes has expanded into its former space.

- **The Owlery and Dervish & Banges** – This is the place to come for your Harry potter wands, as well as more high-end items such as Horcrux replicas to a scaled down model of the Hogwarts Express. Clothing is also sold here, as well as stationary and quick items – you can even bag yourself a golden snitch!
- **The Owl Post** – A real post office where your letters or postcards can be sent to friends and family – these will get a Hogsmeade postmark and a Harry Potter stamp. You will also find stationary on sale here, as well as owl toys.

Note: Official Harry Potter branded wands are expensive – expect to pay at least $35 a piece.

The return ticket system:

J. K. Rowling, the author of the Harry Potter books, specifically requested that the buildings to be made the scale. As such the area is very small and cannot accommodate a huge amount of people.

During periods of high peak attendance you will be required to line up and collect a re-entry ticket with a time slot to enter the land to explore it. This policy is sometimes only be used at certain times of the day and it is impossible to know in advance whether it is being used or not.

It is simply a case of turning up and seeing what is happening at a particular moment. On days with a re-entry ticket system in place, expect very high wait times for all attractions within the land – this is merely a way of limiting the number of people in the land, it is not an Express Pass. When this system is in operation you can usually also opt to stand in a line to get into the *WWOHP* instead – we recommend you do not do this and get a re-entry ticket instead, using the time to explore the rest of the park.

These re-entry tickets are distributed in Jurassic Park and/or The Lost Continent; these are the two lands that lead to the Wizarding World.

Since the opening of the Diagon Alley expansion to the Wizarding

World in Summer 2014, crowds have become more equal across the two parks – as such we do not expect this return ticket system to be used except in the rarest of occasions. Note that this system can also be used at Diagon Alley during peak attendance.

Character Meets:
When discussing the terms for the construction of the land, J.K. Rowling required that there were be no characters to meet in the area – so you will not be able to meet Harry, Hermione, Hagrid, Draco, Ron or any other characters from the films in the Wizarding World.

Early Entry:
Staying on site at a Universal hotel resort has numerous benefits – including, notably, early admission into the WWOHP one hour before the general public. This also applies to off-site hotels booked as part of a Universal vacation package which includes park tickets and accommodation together at www.universalorlandovacations.com or through an authorized reseller – check to make sure this benefit is included in your package.

If you do not have Early Park Admission, be at the park turnstiles well before opening as Universal frequently lets guests in up to 20 minutes earlier than the advertised opening time.

Jurassic Park:

Camp Jurassic
A play area themed around the Jurassic Park films for the little ones to unwind and run around.

Fun fact: Stepping on some of the dinosaur footprints on the ground in this area, will emit a roaring dinosaur sound.

Pteranodon Flyers

Park area: Jurassic Park
Height Restriction: The minimum height is 36 inches (0.92m). Guests over 56 inches (1.43m) must be accompanied by someone under 36 inches (0.92m) to ride.
Attraction length: 1 minute
Express Pass Available: Yes
Average Wait: 45 to 90 minutes

Soar above Jurassic Park on a winged dinosaur. This is the only attraction in the park to have both a minimum and a maximum height restriction that really limits its age range and the people who can experience it. Guests over 56 inches must ride with someone between 36 inches and 56 inches.

Jurassic Park River Adventure

Park area: Jurassic Park
Height Restriction: 42 inches (1.07m)
Capacity: 3000 people per hour.

Attraction length: 5 minutes 30 seconds
Express Pass Available: Yes
Average Wait: 45 to 90 minutes

Step into the world of Jurassic Park on a river boat, glide past huge dinosaurs, enter through the big doors just like in the movies but look out for the T-Rex on the loose as you are sure to come to a splashing end. A single rider line is available at this attraction.

Note: Lockers are not compulsory for this ride, so be prepared to pay $4 for 90 minutes of locker time. There are also giant human-sized dryers priced at around $5 but we find these to be hugely ineffective and a waste of money.

Jurassic Park Discovery Center

An exploration area where you can see models of all different kinds of dinosaurs, play dinosaur-themed carnival-style games, learn about DNA sequencing, and witness a dinosaur birth.

Top Tip: Exit out the back doors and you will find an outdoor patio area which is a great place to take long-shot photos of *Islands of Adventure* – you will get great views of *Seuss Landing* and *Marvel Super Hero Island* in particular.

Restaurants:
The Burger Digs - Quick Service location. Accepts Universal Dining Plan. Serves burgers, chicken tenders and chicken sandwiches. Entrees priced $8 to $10.

Thunder Falls Terrace - Quick Service location. Accepts Universal Dining Plan. Serves cheeseburgers, ribs, smoked turkey legs, wraps, and rotisserie chicken. Entrees priced $9 to $16. The portion sizes are large at this restaurant.

Toon Lagoon:

Dudley Do-Right Ripsaw Falls

Park area: Toon Lagoon
Height Restriction: 44 inches (1.12m)
Attraction length: 7 minutes
Express Pass Available: Yes
Average Wait: 45 to 60 minutes

Want a water ride that gets you absolutely soaked? You should give this a try. The ride contains a well-themed interior and culminates in several drops with a final rollercoaster-esque splashdown making sure you leave thoroughly drenched. The ride reaches a staggering top speed of 45mph (over 70 km/h) meaning you get a great thrill too! A single rider line is available at this attraction.

Me Ship, The Olive

A play area for the kids to run around in. This is usually a very quiet area of the park and a great place to have a break from the crowds. For those who like causing chaos, there are free water cannons on the top level of the ship to spray guests on the water ride below.

Top Tip: The top level of this attraction gives you some great views of the park and is a good place to get photos.

Fun fact: On the right hand side of this attraction there is a trail. Follow it for some hilarious gags, such as a "school" of fish.

Popeye & Bluto's Bilge-Rat Barges

Park area: Toon Lagoon
Height Restriction: 42 inches (1.07m)
Capacity: 2400 people per hour
Attraction length: 6 minutes

Express Pass Available: Yes
Average Wait: 45 to 90 minutes

If you thought you got wet on Dudley Do-Right, you surely have not seen this ride yet. Popeye's will make sure you will come out drenched from head to toe. This is by far the wettest water ride in all of Orlando and it is a whole lot of fun along the way.

Restaurants:
Blondie's - Quick Service location. Accepts Universal Dining Plan. Serves sandwiches, made to order subs and hot dogs. Entrees priced $9 to $9.50.
Comic Strip Cafe - Quick Service location. Accepts Universal Dining Plan. Serves Chinese beef and broccoli, chilidogs, sandwiches, fish & chips, pizza and spaghetti and meatballs. Entrees priced at $7.50 to $14.

Marvel Super Hero Island

The Amazing Adventures of Spider-Man

Park area: Marvel Super Hero Island
Height Restriction: 40 inches (1.02m)
Attraction length: 5 minutes
Express Pass Available: Yes
Average Wait: 45 to 75 minutes

One of the most groundbreaking rides around the world, *Spider-Man* become a world-class attraction which incorporated projection screens with real world elements like no one had seen before. More than a decade later the attraction has not aged a single bit, as it has been updated with 4K 3D technology creating higher resolution images and the storyline works as well as it ever has. The ride, which still wins awards every year to this day, is a fun experience around New York City swinging around with Spider-Man. This is an absolute must-do at the park and is an un-missable experience.

Doctor Doom's Fearfall

Park area: Marvel Super Hero Island
Height Restriction: 52 inches (1.32m)
Capacity: 1600 people per hour
Attraction length: Less than 45 seconds
Express Pass Available: Yes
Average Wait: 45 to 60 minutes

Love drop towers? Then you will adore this ride. Doctor Doom needs your screams for power, so the logical thing to do is to shoot you up in the air and collect them as you scream your lungs out in fear.

Fun fact: Look on the ground outside of the attraction for chalk outlines of the Fantastic Four. The Idea is that they too went on the ride and came plummeting to the ground, landing where the outlines are. A subtle feature, but really cool.

The Incredible Hulk Coaster

Park area: Marvel Super Hero Island
Height Restriction: 54 inches (1.37m)
Capacity: 1920 people per hour
Attraction length: 2 minutes 15 seconds
Express Pass Available: Yes.
Average Wait: 30 to 90 minutes

Winner of numerous awards, the Incredible Hulk Coaster is our favorite rollercoaster in all of Orlando and perhaps in the world. It is a truly outstanding thrill with huge loops, an underground section, and non-stop fun from the moment you are launched out of the tunnel. There is a hidden single rider line at this attraction which you must ask the attendant at the front to use – it is very often empty as it is not signposted.

Storm Force Accelatron

Park area: Marvel Super Hero Island
Height Restriction: An adult must accompany those under 48 inches (1.22m).
Attraction length: 2 minutes
Express Pass Available: Yes
Average Wait: Less than 15 minutes

A standard teacup style ride themed to Marvel super hero, Storm.

Restaurants:
Captain America Diner - Quick Service location. Accepts Universal Dining Plan. Serves cheeseburgers, chicken sandwiches, chicken fingers and salads. Entrees priced $8 to $10.50.
Cafe 4 - Quick Service location. Accepts Universal Dining Plan. Serves pizza, pasta, sandwiches and salads. Entrees priced $6 to $9.

Entertainment:
There are no fireworks shows or parades at this park. You will often find characters throughout the various lands, in particular in Seuss Landing and Marvel Superhero Island.

Chapter 7
Universal CityWalk:

Universal's CityWalk is located just outside the theme parks and is located nearby to all the on-site hotels - in order to get into and out of the resort you must make at least two trips through this area of shops, restaurants, bars, cinemas and clubs.

Unlike *Downtown Disney/Disney Springs*, *CityWalk* has more of an adult feel to it, particularly at nighttime where there is a heavy focus on the club-like atmosphere. It by no means feels unsafe, however, and is a perfectly family friendly environment. Like *Downtown Disney/Disney Springs*, there is no admission required to enter *CityWalk* - anyone can explore the area for free.

To get specifics on restaurant and attraction operating hours, as well as any other information recorded information is available by calling (407) 363-8000.

Guest Services is well signposted and is located next to the **restrooms**. Also located nearby is **First Aid**.

From CityWalk you can catch complimentary boats to and from the deluxe on-site resort hotels, and can walk to all on-site hotels. Room keys are not usually necessary to board the boat service but these may be asked for during the late hours.

Dining:

CityWalk is filled with unique dining experiences allowing you to have a taste of Italy, New Orleans, Jamaica and the US all in one place. This section helps you choose where you should visit on your next visit. Note that entrée prices quoted in this section are for adult meals; children's meals will often be significantly cheaper.

There are numerous quick service dining options:

Breadbox – Accepts Universal Dining Plan. Serves sandwiches and salads. Entrees priced at $6 to $8.

Burger King 'Whopper Bar' - Does not accept Universal Dining Plan. Serves burgers, wraps and sandwiches.

Cold Stone Creamery - Accepts Universal Dining Plan for selected snacks. Serves ice cream.

Cinnabon – Accepts Universal Dining Plan for selected snacks and beverages only. Serves cinnamon rolls and ice cream. Ice creams priced at $5 to $9.50.

Fusion Bistro Sushi & Sake Bar – Does not accept Universal Dining Plan. Serves

Hot Dog Hall of Fame – Accepts Universal Dining Plan. Serves hot dogs. Entress priced at $7 to $13.

Menchie's Frozen Yogurt - Accepts Universal Dining Plan. Serves frozen yogurt priced at $0.59 per ounce (28g).

Moe's Southwest Grill - Does not accept Universal Dining Plan. Serves burritos, tacos, fajitas and other southwest dishes. Entrees priced at $4 to $8.50.

Panda Express – Does not accept Universal Dining Plan. Serves Chinese food.

Red Oven Pizza Bakery – Accepts Universal Dining Plan. Serves pizza and salads. Whole pies priced at $12 to $14. Hands down the best pizza at Universal Orlando.

Starbucks Coffee – Accepts Universal Dining Plan for selected snacks and beverages only. Serves coffees, ice-based drinks, sandwiches and pastries.

There are many table service dining options at CityWalk:

Antojitos Authentic Mexican Food – Accepts Universal Dining Plan. Serves Mexican-style food. Entrees priced at $14 to $20. There is also an "Up" section to the restaurant located upstairs – entrees here are priced at $14 to $29.

Bob Marley – A Tribute to Freedom – Accepts Universal Dining Plan. Serves Jamaican-style dishes. Entrees priced at $9 to $17.

Bubba Gump Shrimp Co – Does not accept Universal Dining Plan. Serves seafood and other dishes. Entrees priced at $11 to $27.

The Cowfish Sushi Burger bar – Does not accept Universal Dining Plan. Serves burgers and sushi. Entrees priced at $10 to $27.

Emeril's Restaurant Orlando – Does not accept Universal Dining Plan. Serves Louisiana-style food. Entrees priced at $11 to $39.

Hard Rock Cafe Orlando – Does not accept Universal Dining Plan. Serves burgers, steaks, ribs and other American-style food. Entrees priced at $10 to $35.

Jimmy Buffet's Margaritaville - Accepts Universal Dining Plan. Serves Floridian and Caribbean inspired food. Entrees priced at $11 to $39.

NBA City – Accepts Universal Dining Plan. Serves American style food. Entrees priced at $10 to $34.

Pat O' Briens – Accepts Universal Dining Plan. A music venue that serves some food. Serves New Orleans-style dishes. Entrees priced at $10 to $15.

Vivo Italian Kitchen – Accepts Universal Dining Plan. Serves Italian food. Entrees priced at $11 to $33.

Reservations for table service establishments can be made by calling (407) 224-3663 on by visiting opentable.com. Emeril's reservations are made directly by calling (407) 224-2424. Hard Rock Café Orlando priority seating can be requested online.

If you want to combine a meal at select locations with a Party Pass (more information on this later) you can do so for about $21 including tax and gratuity.

A meal plus mini-golf deal is also available for about $4 including tax and gratuity, and includes a meal at one of the select CityWalk locations, and 18 holes of mini-golf at the Hollywood Drive-In course.

Top Tip 1: Most establishments have happy hours throughout the day and evening when drinks and snacks can be obtained at significant discounts. These vary from location to location so simply ask the staff for details.

Top Tip 2: Want free CityWalk valet parking? Most restaurants will validate your ticket for a 2-hour stay between the hours of 11:00am to 2:00pm Monday to Friday. Emeril's will validate your ticket at any time. Tipping the valets is still required.

Movie theatre/cinema:

CityWalk features an AMC Universal Cineplex with 20 screens, including one that shows films in IMAX and IMAX 3D.

Tickets prices vary depending on the time of day and several other factors. A general ticket for an adult is priced at $9.75 for shows before 3:55pm and $11.50 from then onwards. Children pay $8.75 all day. "AM" Cinema showings on weekends and holidays before midday are $6.50. Senior tickets for those aged 60 and over are charged at $10.50 (but only $6.50 on Tuesdays) and students pay $8.75 all day on Thursdays with a valid student ID.

There are upcharges for non-standard tickets. These are: an additional $4 for a 3D movie, $5 for IMAX and $6 for IMAX-3D.

Annual pass holders get $3 off two tickets for showings after 4:00pm.

You can save by combining a standard movie ticket and a meal at select CityWalk restaurants. The price is $21.95 including tax and gratuity.

Mini Golf:
"Hollywood Drive-In Golf" is an adventure golf location with two different courses - one themed to sci-fi ("Invaders from Planet Putt"), the other themed to horror movies ("The Haunting of Ghostly Greens"). The sounds, special effects, lighting and theming truly immerse you in the miniature world you are in. The price for one course is $15 per adult and $13 per child. A single course will take between 35 and 45 minutes to complete with each being made up of 18 holes. The entrance is located next to the AMC Cineplex box office.

If you play both courses you will receive a T-shirt as a souvenir.

The mini-golf location is open from 9:00am to 2:00am daily.

Top Tip: Get your mini-golf tickets in advance at http://www.hollywooddriveingolf.com and save up to 13% per ticket– you must book these at least one day in advance.

Nighttime entertainment - Blue Man Group:

The world famous *Blue Man Group* is the staple nighttime show at Universal. The Blue Men create live music with makeshift instruments in a fun, hilarious musical adventure.

The best seats can be had as close to the front as possible and towards the center. The show lasts 1 hour 45 minutes and has no interval. Show schedules change daily with no fixed start times and there are between 1 and 3 shows per day, with shows starting between 3:00pm and 9:00pm.

Ticket prices vary depending on the day of the week. The following prices (tax excluded) are valid from Sunday to Thursday – add $10 per adult and $5 per child for Friday and Saturday shows. Higher prices also apply daily during peak seasons.

	Tier 1	Tier 2	Poncho	Premium
Adult	$70	$85	$95	$105
Child	$30	$37.50	$42.50	$47.50

A VIP experience is available for an additional supplement of $20 per ticket. It includes 2 drinks (alcoholic or non-alcoholic), access to the Bluephoria lounge 45 minutes before and after the show, a meet and greet with a Blue Man and a signed photo.

Tickets can be purchased at the box office or by calling 407-BLUEMAN (407-258-3626) or online at www.blueman.com. Pre-purchasing tickets can save you up to $10 per ticket. An Annual Passholder discount is available with tickets starting at $60 for adults and $30 for children, plus tax.

Money-Saving Top Tips: Students with a college ID or an ISIC card can get "rush" day-of tickets for $34 – there is a limit of two per ID. AAA members can get a discount by showing their membership card. Military members can also get a discount, visit your local MWR, ITT, and ITR offices for details and to purchase.

Shopping:
If you fancy a spot of shopping there are plenty of places to visit too including: Fossil, Fresh Produce, Quiet Flight Surf Shop, Element, The Island Clothing Store, a large Universal Studios Store (get theme park gear without having to enter the theme parks) and Katie's Candy Company. Finally, if you are in the mood for a tattoo then Hart & Huntington Tattoo Company is the place for you!

Universal CityWalk Nightlife
As far as bars nightclubs are concerned you will find Red Coconut Club, Pat O' Briens, CityWalk's Rising Star, the groove and Fat Tuesday. You will also find live music played at Hard Rock Live Orlando. Lone Palm Airport is an outdoor bar just across from Jimmy Buffet's.

If you fancy partying the night away then you may want to take advantage of the $11.99 *CityWalk* Party Pass (annual Passholders get 20% off for up to 4 people) which allows you unlimited one-night access to all of the following locations:
- CityWalk's Rising Star
- Jimmy Buffett's Margaritaville
- the groove
- Pat O'Brien's
- Red Coconut Club
- Bob Marley – A Tribute to Freedom

Note: A party pass will not allow you entry when special ticketed events are taking place in a nightclub.

If you do not own a Party Pass, the cover charge for a single nightclub is $7 and entertainment usually begins at 9:00pm. Hard Rock Café does not have a cover charge.

Top Tip: If you turn up before 9:00pm you will often be able to get in to these locations and not have to pay a cover charge.

If you would like to upgrade for about $4 more you can get the *CityWalk* Party Pass + Movie ticket which allows you entry to all the aforementioned locations plus entry into one movie on the same day! This can be purchased at Guest Services.

Multi-day tickets and Flextickets include a free Party Pass that is valid for 14 days from first admission to the parks. So, multi-day ticket holders will not need to spend any extra to enjoy the nightlife.

Chapter 8
Things for the little ones:

It is hard to imagine Universal Orlando as being a place for small kids when you have rides such as *The Incredible Hulk Coaster* and *Dr. Doom's Fear Fall* dominating the skyline. It is by no means anything like the mouse-run theme parks a few miles down the road, but Universal has not completely forgotten about the smallest members of the family. Both theme parks have areas dedicated especially to children.

Important: Unlike Walt Disney World, baby formula and diapers are not sold at the parks.

Universal Studios Florida:
The small members of the family will enjoy seeing Gru and the gang at *Despicable Me: Minion Mayhem* in a 3D simulator ride. *E.T. Adventure* can be a little dark but is a relaxing ride though kids may not enjoy the sensation of flying. *Woody Woodpecker's Nuthouse Coaster* is a gentle rollercoaster for starters and the surrounding play areas in *Woody Woodpecker's KidZone* are great fun for kids, such as the nearby *Curious George Goes To Town* play area.

For entertainment, kids are sure to love *A Day in the Park with Barney* - a live interactive stage show featuring the dinosaur himself.

When they are happy with these kinds of rides they may want to have a go on *The Simpsons Ride* and see some great characters (note this may be scary due to the immersion through the huge screen and simulator).

Islands of Adventure:

In *Islands of Adventure* kids will be sure to love the *Seuss Landing* area of the park with its bright colors, play areas and meet and greets, as well as several rides which are suitable for all ages including the *Caro-Seuss-el; The Cat in the Hat; One Fish, two Fish, Red Fish, Blue Fish;* and *The High in the Sky Seuss Trolley Train Ride.* In the *Toon lagoon* area you will also find several water play areas for kids (or adults) to splash around in. *Marvel Super Hero Island* also features *Storm Force Accelatron*, which essentially is just a themed teacup ride.

The *Jurassic Park Discovery Centre* can also be a fun and educational place to take kids to learn about dinosaurs.

Once the kids get a little bigger but are not yet ready to brave the likes of the Hulk you can visit *Pteranodon Flyers, Flight of the Hippogriff* and *The Amazing Adventures of Spider-Man.*

Chapter 9
Services:

Photo Connect Star Card Package:

On-ride photos can be expensive souvenirs, especially when we are all capable of printing photos ourselves at home or at a local supermarket or photo store. No one really wants to pay $20 or $30 for a single photo, no matter how good the experience. Now, Universal has the perfect solution with the *Photo Connect Star Card*. After you have ridden your first attraction that takes an on-ride photo, you should visit the photo purchasing location and ask to purchase the *Star Card package*.

The Star Card package is a card on a lanyard which you scan any time you have your photo taken – all these photos are automatically uploaded to the Photo Connect website where you can later download them at full resolution.

To add to the deal, it is not merely ride photos that are included as your character photos and in-park photographer photos are included all on the same card at no extra cost!

The price of the Star Card Package is currently $69.95 plus tax for three consecutive days of photos. In addition, you will get access to the 'Amazing Pictures' app which allows you to view your photos on your iOS or Android smartphone, discounts on in-park ride photo prints, and you will also be entitled to one photo print at the time of the purchase of the Star Card Package.

If you pre-order online, and only if you pre-order online you will also have the option of the one day and fourteen day Star Cards. These are priced at $39.95 and $89.99 respectively.

Annual pass holders can pay $99.95 plus tax and have photos for the duration of their pass. This quickly pays for itself considering the price of prints!

One unadvertised feature of the Star Card is that you can add unlimited photos from Wet n' Wild water park to your account for $20 when you arrive at the water park. Make sure to keep your Star Card with you at all times.

Top Tip: Save $10 on your Star Card packages by buying before you go at https://presale.amazingpictures.com/PhotoConnect.aspx.

As well as the Star Cars packages, which are the best value option, you can also simply go up to any photographer and get an in-park photo. This will be added to a Photo Connect card that you can then use throughout the day at both theme parks. Before the end of the day visit one of the Photo Connect stores and you can then choose the best pictures and have them printed out for you. You will need a new Photo Connect card for each day of your vacation, unless you purchase the Star Card package. All in-park photos will be deleted at the end of the operating day.

Important note: Although superficially the system seems to be fairly similar to Disney's Photopass system we do have one warning – there are nowhere near as many photographers around the parks. You will usually find one at the entrance to each park and then one at some of the character meet and greets, as well as the on-ride photos of course.

Ride Lockers:

Many of the rides at Universal do not allow you to take your belongings with you on them; instead any loose articles must be placed in free lockers. Here is how they work: You approach a locker station, select 'Rent a locker' from the touch screen, put your fingerprint on the reader and you will be assigned a locker to put your stuff in. Go to the locker, put your belongings inside and press the green button next to the locker to lock the door. It is very important that you do this to make sure the locker is actually locked! If you forget to press the green button, it will automatically lock 5 seconds after the door is closed.

The lockers will be free for a certain period of time - this is usually just longer than the current posted attraction wait time. For example, a 90-minute queue for *The* Hulk would typically allow you 100 or 110 minutes of locker rental time to allow you to queue, experience the ride and collect your belongings.

If you keep your stuff in the lockers longer than the free period, charges apply – the charge is $3 for each additional 30 minutes, up to a maximum daily charge of $20.

Lockers for the water rides are unusually not free and are priced at $4 for the duration of the ride, and $3 for each additional 30 minutes, up to a maximum daily charge of $20.

List of rides with lockers:

Top tip 1: If you rented a locker and your free time has expired because the line took longer than expected, tell a team member who will sort out the issue.

Top tip 2: If you forget your locker number there is a feature that will help you find it.

Top tip 3: Lockers for water rides are not free; a walk to a locker at a ride where they are free can save you a significant amount of money over the course of a trip. *Forbidden Journey* often has long locker rental times for example.

Top tip 4: The touchscreens on these lockers are terrible, meaning that you will more than likely find it hard to use your fingers as the lockers often will not register your touches. We recommend using you fingernail or your knuckles to touch the screen to solve this problem.

All-day park locker rentals:
Non-ride specific lockers are located by the entrance to each park - the cost is $8 per day for a standard locker or $10 per day for a family size locker (only at *Universal Studios Florida*). Guests may access these lockers as many times as they want throughout the day, though location can be quite a pain as they are not centrally located.

Universal Express Pass:

If you do not find waiting in line hugely enjoyable (and let's face it, who does?) and are willing to pay to get on rides quicker, then Universal's Express Pass system is just the system for you. The system is free for those staying on-site at Universal deluxe hotels and can cost anywhere from $39 to $139 per day per person otherwise. Essentially it is a card that allows you to skip the regular lines at almost every attraction and enter a separate line which will be significantly shorter and drastically reduce your wait time. For shows, you will be allowed entry before guests who do not have an Express Pass – usually 15 minutes before the show is due to begin.

Which rides are not included?
Express Passes are valid on all attractions at both theme parks with the following exceptions: *Harry Potter and The Forbidden Journey*, *Ollivander's Wand Shop (Hogsmeade)* and *Pteranodon Flyers* in Universal's Islands of Adventure. At Universal Studios Florida, *Kang & Kodos' Twirl 'n' Hurl*, *Hogwarts Express (both stations)*, *Ollivander's Wand Shop (Diagon Alley)* and *Harry Potter and The Escape from Gringotts* do not offer Express Pass access.

How do I use it?
When at an attraction simply show your Express Pass to the Team Member at the ride entrance, they will scan it and you will be directed to a separate queue line from non-Express Pass guests. Typically waits will be 15 minutes or less for rides even on the busiest days – often much less. Despicable Me: Minion Mayhem often has a wait that is longer than 15 minutes in the Express Pass line due to its slow loading nature.

Be aware that because you will be in a different queue line to the main one, Express Pass guests may lose some of the storyline told in the queue. This is particularly evident on *Revenge of the Mummy*, *Transformers* and *Men in Black*.

There are three types of Express Pass:
- **Universal Express Pass:** This is available for purchase both in the parks and online in advance. It allows one ride per participating attraction.
- **Universal Express Unlimited:** This is available for purchase online and in the parks. It allows unlimited rides on each participating attraction.
- **Park-To-Park Ticket + Universal Express Unlimited**: This is available for purchase online or over the phone (407-224-7840) and includes a regular park admission ticket for both parks and Universal Express Unlimited access for each day's entry – these tickets are available in one-day or multiple day versions. The ticket will expire when all park admission days on the ticket are used or 14 days after first use, whichever is

sooner.

- **On-site Hotel Universal Express Unlimited Pass:** This is a perk for on-site hotel guests (excluding Cabana Bay Resort guests) and is included for each member of a party staying in the hotel room for every day of their stay including through all of the check in day and all of their check out day. It allows unlimited rides on each attraction. A photo of each guest will be printed onto this pass.

Each member of your party will need their own Express Pass. If you are not using an "On-site Hotel Universal Express Unlimited Pass" or a "Park-To-Park Ticket + Universal Express Unlimited" you will need to purchase a separate Express Pass for each day of your trip. There is no such thing as a multi-day Express Pass. In addition, you will need to have an Express Pass for each member of your party.

Do I need an Express Pass?

In our opinion, during extremely busy periods getting an Express Pass is almost essential to your visit. It will make sure that you will not need to wait hours upon hours in line especially if you are limited to a short visit of a day or a day and a half. Admittedly, the Express Passes are expensive and will often double the price of your admission. Having said this, will careful planning and by following our touring plans chapter you should be able to do all the rides you want each day.

If you are visiting for multiple days you should be able to do all the attractions in three full days at the parks and therefore an Express Pass is not a necessity but you may wish to consider getting one day of Express to begin with, and then repeating attractions at a more leisurely pace on your other days without an Express Pass.

If you will be visiting outside of the peak periods of school breaks and public holidays, then the chances are that an Express Pass will be a waste of money. Outside of peak periods you should not need to wait more than 30 minutes for most attractions though if you want to do both parks in one day then an Express Pass will still be needed.

Finally, if you are going to get an Express Pass we recommend you get the 'Unlimited' version – there is no point in paying extra to skip attractions and then only being able to do this once per ride. If you enjoy a ride, getting the Unlimited version of the Express pass means that you can instantly re-ride it.

Ultimately, if you cannot afford it, do not purchase an Express Pass. The money you spend on it can usually be used to feed your family in the parks all day and get several souvenirs. You will not miss out by not getting an Express Pass if you invest the time to get up early and follow our touring plans – yes you will wait longer in line than without an Express Pass but you will potentially save hundreds of dollars in the process too.

Top tip 1: Careful planning will allow you to know when rides will have the longest queues and save you time.

Top tip 2: Do not buy Express Passes in advance, there is no real benefit to this and the park may not be busy when you visit. However, Express Passes do sell out so there is the potential that there will be none when you arrive, particularly if you visit during a peak period of the year.

Top tip 3: There is an Express Pass kiosk outside the park gates - do not use it. Go inside the park and see how long the queue times are first - if you can manage them, go and enjoy your day. If not, you can buy the Express Pass inside the park, usually with a shorter queue lines than outside.

Top tip 4: Holders of the top-tier annual pass get complimentary Express Pass access after 4:00pm.

Top Tip 5: During certain periods of the year there are Post-4:00pm Express Passes on sale for only $36 – these are of course infinitely more valuable when the park is open until 10:00pm rather than 6:00pm. You will need to ask for these specifically as they will not be listed in advance.

Top Tip 6: The "Park-To-Park Ticket + Universal Express Unlimited" ticket bundle works out cheaper than purchasing park admission and Universal Express Unlimited access separately.

Top Tip 7: If you are staying on-site and get a free Hotel Express Pass, this only applies during regular park hours. During extra-hours events where a separate admission ticket is required such as Halloween Horror Nights you will need to purchase an event-specific Express Pass.

Top Tip 8: For a group of people it is often cheaper to get an on-site deluxe hotel for one night allowing you Express Pass access for two days, rather than buying Express Passes for each person.

Single Rider:

One of the best ways to significantly reduce your time waiting in queue lines is to use the Single Rider line instead of the regular queue line. Essentially this is a completely separate queue line that is used to fill free spaces on ride vehicles. For example if a ride vehicle can seat 8 people and a group of 4 turns up, and then a group of 3 takes the other seats, then a 'single rider' will fill the empty space on the ride vehicle instead of that space going round empty. This ultimately makes the wait times shorter for everyone in the park as all spaces are utilized.

If the park does get extremely busy then sometimes single rider lines can be closed - this happens when the wait in the single rider line is the same or greater than the regular line, thereby undermining its purpose. If the park is almost empty then sometimes these lines do not operate, as there is no need for them.

Some rides do not have an obviously signposted Single Rider line - in this case simply ask the first attraction host you see (usually at the entrance to the attraction) if Single Rider is operating. If it is, then they will direct you accordingly. One prime example of this is *The Incredible Hulk Coaster* that does not advertise its single rider line - you have to ask for it. The *Harry Potter and the Forbidden Journey* single rider line can also be easily missed if you do not ask for it at the entrance.

If you are travelling as part of a group, you can still use the Single Rider line – just be aware that, as the name indicates, you will not ride with each other but you can still meet each other at the exit of the ride after the ride has finished.

Single rider lines are available on: *The Incredible Hulk, The Amazing Adventures of Spiderman, Harry Potter and the Forbidden Journey, Jurassic Park River Adventure, Dr. Doom's Fearfall, Dudley Do-Right's Ripsaw Falls, Transformers: The Ride, Hollywood Rip Ride Rockit, Revenge of the Mummy, Harry Potter and the Escape from Gringotts,* and *Men in Black: Alien Attack.*

Child Swap:

Sometimes attractions are not suitable for children – Universal Orlando has a timesaving solution. If there are two adults going to the park and they both want to go on a ride which is not suitable for children but they have a child with them, there could be a problem. Each would have to take it in turns with the child, and the parents would each need to queue up doubling their wait time. However, Universal has a solution – Child Swap. This can also happen when a kid *is* tall enough, but just does not want to ride.

Simply go up to a Team Member an attraction entrance and ask to use Child Swap, each ride works a little differently but generally one or more adults will go in the standard queue line while another adult is directed to a child swap waiting area. Once the first group rides the attraction, they will be directed to the Child Swap area. Here the first group will stay with the child, and the person who originally sat with the child gets to ride straight away, without having to wait. This procedure may vary from attraction to attraction – make sure you ask the first Universal Team Member you at an attraction about the specific procedure.

Q-Bot Ride reservation system:

Universal's ride reservation scheme is billed as a more affordable alternative to Express Pass. The system can be purchased anywhere that Express Pass can be purchased and is valid on all Express Pass rides, but it can not be used for shows.

How it works:
Unlike the Express Pass, this system does not get you onto rides any faster; instead it allows you to virtually reserve a place in line. For example: The time is currently 14:00 and the line for *Revenge of the Mummy* is 40 minutes. You select *Revenge of the Mummy* on your Q-Bot and you will make a reservation – in this example that reservation will be for 14:40 (the current time plus the time you would have spent in line). At 14:40 you can return to the attraction and you will be allowed into the Express Pass line – this line will get you onto the ride quicker but may take up to 15 minutes during busy periods of the year.

Until that time you could go and experience another attraction or show in the regular line, go shopping, get something to eat, etc. One great feature of the Q-Bot is that you can make your ride reservations anywhere on the device and do not have to be physically present at that attraction to reserve – this means for example that you could be having lunch and make a reservation for *Despicable Me Minion Mayhem* for example.

Cancelling reservations:

You may cancel reservations at any time, but you may only have one ride reservation at a time. In order to create another reservation you must experience the ride or cancel a reservation. Going back to our previous example, you can ride *Revenge of the Mummy* any time after 14:40. If it is 14:45 and you have still not used your RoTM reservation, you cannot book another ride reservation until you use the *RoTM* reservation or cancel it. Do not cancel your reservation as you walk up to the ride, the attendant will do that for you.

What are my options?
There are two versions of the system like the Express Pass - one provides one reservation per ride, the other provides unlimited reservations per ride meaning that you can make multiple reservations for the same ride after one another.

Is it worth it?
Given the option of Express Passes and the Q-Bot and an unlimited supply of money, of course the Express Passes win as you will be on a ride within a maximum of 15 minutes – and usually in less than 5 minutes. However, if you have a more limited budget and do not like waiting in long lines then this could be the perfect system for you.

Theoretically you will not need to queue at all for rides as you make reservations, and use that time instead to watch shows, shop, dine and meet characters. In reality though, the Q-Bot will simply allow you to double the number of attractions you do as you use the normal queue line for one, and make a reservation for another. To get the most out of this system we recommend making Q-Bot reservations for the rides with the longest waits instead of several with shorter waits.

If you are visiting both parks in one day and want to skip the lines at both, then the Q-Bot is unlikely to be a good option as you will need to purchase one Q-Bot at each park which is a lot of hassle and becoming tiresome – we recommend an Express Pass in this case despite the extra cost.

Note 1: There is no two-park version of this system, it can only be purchased for one park - if you want to use it for a second park then you must purchase it separately.

Note 2: Q-Bot is not necessarily offered every day of the year. There are times when only Express Passes are sold instead.

Note 3: When you purchase access to a Q-Bot you will receive a voucher which will need to be exchanged elsewhere inside the park. There you will pay sign a contract stating you will return it and provide credit or debit card payment details. You cannot use the Q-Bot system without a credit or debit card. If the Q-Bot is not returned or is damaged, then you will be charged a $50 fee per Q-Bot.

Internet access:

Sometimes you need to stay connected whilst on vacation, and internet access has become almost indispensable over the past few years – whether you need to send a business email, check the route to your next destination, book a hotel, check your credit card bill or upload a photo to Instagram. Theme parks have started offering complimentary Wi-Fi access over the past couple of years, beginning with Walt Disney World, and in 2014 this service finally reached the Universal Orlando resort.

You can find free Wi-Fi throughout both theme parks and the CityWalk area to connect to. The network to connect to is simply called "Universal". As Xfinity sponsors the Wi-Fi, Xfinity customers can simply log-in with their account credentials. Non-Xfinity customers still have access to free Wi-Fi upon providing their zip code and email address.

In-room Wi-Fi access is offered at no cost to hotel guests for the "standard" level – if you require higher speed access there is a "premium" option available for $15 per day. The lobby and pool areas in all the on-site hotels have free Wi-Fi which you can access regardless of whether you are staying at the hotel.

The Universal Orlando app:

'The Official Universal Orlando Resort App' available for free on smartphones allows you to access wait times for all attractions when inside the parks, get directions to attractions with a step-by-step visual representation, see upcoming show times and special events, be alerted when a wait time drops below a certain figure, see park and resort maps, find guest amenities, see park hours, set show time alerts, social sharing, and locate food items.

Universal Orlando is also promising that in future it will add new features such as instant Express Pass purchase (even in queue lines!) and customizable itineraries to be made. The App is available for free on the Apple App Store and the Google Play store.

Package delivery:

One great service that many theme parks offer to their guests is package delivery and Universal is no exception. Essentially, this allows you to purchase an item and then have it stored until later in the day when you can pick it up, without having to carry it around with you all day. There two places you can have your package sent to are:

- **The front of the park** - Just by each of the theme parks' exit turnstiles you will see a small shop that is accessible both from inside and outside the park. Purchases you have made throughout the day will be sent here for you to pick up later.

Please allow up to 4 hours for delivery to this window.

- **Your hotel room** - You can also have the package delivered straight to your hotel room if you are staying at any of the Universal on-site hotels. The only caveat is that it will be delivered the next day between 9:00am and 4:00pm. Therefore this service is unavailable the day before checkout or the day of checkout itself so it is really only suitable for stays of 3 nights or longer.

Stroller and Wheelchair Rental:

Both theme parks offer stroller and wheelchair rental, as well as the rental of ECVs. The rental area is located to the left hand side of each park's turnstiles.

There are four main types of strollers you can rent:
*Single Stroller - $15 per day
*Single Kiddie Car - $18 per day
*Double Stroller - $25 per day
*Double Kiddie Car - $28 per day

Wheelchairs can be rented for $12 per day, plus a $50 deposit.
ECVs can be rented for $50 per day, plus a $50 deposit.

The difference between a stroller and a kiddie car is that the kiddie car is designed to look like a car instead of a regular stroller with a enclosed front foot area making it harder for kids to slip out, and a steering wheel for kids to play with.

ECVs must be operated by a single person aged 18 years old or over.

Wheelchairs can also be rented in the parking rotunda area.

Chapter 10
Guests with disabilities:

Visiting a theme park with a disability can seem like a complicated process, but whatever your disability Universal Orlando has worked hard to make your experience as positive as possible and to give you as much of the experience as they can. Although, we could not possibly cover every kind of disability in this section we have tried to include as much information as is possible.

Universal Attraction Assistance Pass:
A Universal Attraction Assistance Pass can really ease the day for some visitors. In order to obtain it you will need to go to Guest Services (to the right through the turnstiles) and ask for the Attraction Assistance Pass.

Although it is not required, we strongly recommend you get a note from your doctor in English explaining what exactly you need help with - whether it is not waiting in the sun to not waiting for prolonged periods of time in line to not waiting in crowded areas. It will all depend on your situation. Your doctor does NOT need to explain what your disability is, merely what help you will require in the theme parks.

The Universal Team Members at Guest Services will ask you several question to determine eligibility and what type of help you will need – as mentioned before a letter from a doctor is not required, but will greatly assist this process. You will then be issued an Attraction Assistance Pass and it will be explained to you.

Using the pass:

When you reach an attraction you would like to experience, show your Assistance Pass to the first Team Member you see at the entrance of the line (this person is called the attraction 'greeter'). If the regular attraction wait time is less than 30 minutes then you will be immediately directed towards an alternative queue - this is often the Express Pass queue line. If the regular wait time for the attraction is more than 30 minutes then the greeter will write down a time on your Pass to return – we will call this a 'reservation' for the purpose of this guide. When that time comes around, show your pass with the reservation written in it at the ride entrance and you will be allowed entry through the alternative queue. Remember that this is NOT a front-of-the-line ticket and waits will be up to 15 minutes.

You can only hold one 'reservation' for a ride with a wait of over 30 minutes at any one time. You may still enjoy accelerated entrance to attractions with less than a 30-minute wait even if you have a reservation. If you want to change which attraction you have a reservation for simply go to the next attraction and make a reservation with the attraction's greeter at the entrance - this will automatically void your previous reservation. An Assistance Pass allows up to 25 reservations which should be more than enough for a single day.

The Assistance Pass will be valid for up to 6 people in the person's party.

Express Guest Assistance Pass:
The Express Guest Assistance Pass is used in situations where waiting in any form of long queue or having to return later is simply not possible and therefore the classic Universal Attractions Assistance Pass is not suitable – as such it is for a much more limited number of guests and is more difficult to obtain. This Pass once again does not requires proof from a doctor's note but it can really help in this situation. You may need to ask to speak to a manager to obtain this card.

Generally speaking the Express Guest Assistance Pass is for guests with certain mental health disorders, though a full list is not disclosed. This Pass will allow you to enter the alternative queue instantly without the return time wait. However, this is NOT a front-of-the-line ticket and you must wait in the alternative queue. The Express GAP is not valid at *Harry Potter and the Escape from Gringotts* and *the Hogwarts Express* at Universal Studios Florida. It is also not valid at *Harry Potter and the Forbidden Journey, the Hogwarts Express, and Pteranodon Flyers* at Islands of Adventure. If you wish to visit the above rides, then a classic Attraction Assistance Pass will be needed as well or you will need to use the normal queue line instead. Overall, this Pass acts very similarly to the Universal Express Pass Unlimited.

Other accommodations for disabled guests:
Deaf/Hard of Hearing - For guests who are deaf or hard of hearing, many in-park shows have interpreted performances. These are printed on the park map. Closed captioning and assistive listening devices, guidebooks for guests with disabilities, and attraction scripts are available at Guest Services in each theme park as well.

Mobility Impairment and wheelchairs - The whole of Universal Orlando has been designed to be as wheelchair-accessible as possible with ramps instead of steps and all shopping and dining facilities being accessible. Guests who would like to use a stroller as a wheelchair should ask for a special tag from Guest Services.

Outdoor stage shows also have areas designed for wheelchair users and their parties. Rides are accessible - some will require a transfer, others will allow you to ride in your wheelchair.

You can get a wheelchair at the parking rotunda to help with the considerable distance from the rotunda to the theme parks if necessary – simply ask the Team Members here. Alternatively you can rent these inside the theme parks.

Guests may pay the additional cost for an ECV once at the theme park or continue to use the wheelchair throughout the day.

Note you do not NEED to have an Attraction Assistance Pass if you are in a wheelchair as all rides have an accessible entrance, but it can make things easier when there are particularly long queues so we do recommend it. If you or someone you are with suffers from a disability that is not easily seen we thoroughly recommend the use of one of the Assistance Passes as the attraction greeters will most likely make you use the regular queue due to company procedures.

Service Animals are permitted throughout the theme parks but each attraction will have a specific way of boarding. Kennels exist at some attractions for service animals. The greeters at the entry of each attraction will be able to provide more information.

Rides and shows:
Additionally special requirements exist for guests with prosthetic limbs and guests with oxygen tanks. More information about rides and shows specifically is available through the Riders Guide for Rider Safety & Guests with Disabilities (PDF file). It can be downloaded online from
http://www.universalorlando.com/Images/Riders_Guide_tcm13-26195.pdf

Chapter 11

Dining:

When visiting Universal Orlando you will find an abundance of choice of food from standard theme park fare to more exotic tastes. Eating in a theme park you have never visited for the first time can be daunting, so this chapter will reveal all.

At Universal you are able to walk into quick-service (fast-food style) places and get food within a few minutes, get food and drinks from snack carts throughout the parks or opt for a full sit down meal. You can even eat whilst characters come round and meet and greet at your tables and pose for photos.

All these can be experienced by showing up and paying on the door but Universal also offers programs to help those who like to plan in advance, the dining plans.

Quick Service Universal Dining Plan

The Quick Service Universal Dining Plan is available to all guests at Universal and can be bought in the theme park at any Quick Service location, online at UniversalOrlando.com or at dining reservation kiosks in the parks. It is accepted at over 100 locations at the Universal Orlando Resort (although *Leaky Cauldron* is notably excluded).

The cost of the quick service dining plan is $19.99 + tax for adults and $12.99 + tax per child.

Each day purchased on the Universal Quick Service Dining Plan entitles you to:

1 Quick Service meal - with Entree and Non-alcoholic beverage.

2 Snacks - From food carts or quick service locations such as popcorn, ice cream or a frozen beverage.
1 Non-Alcoholic Beverage - From food carts or quick service locations.

Guests who purchase the Quick Service Dining Plan in advance must pick up their dining plan card with their credits to use the scheme. You will receive a voucher when you have booked your dining plan that can be exchanged in the theme parks or *CityWalk*. The voucher can be exchanged for a card at the Ticket Centre Desk at either theme park, Guest Services at either theme park or the Dining Reservation Cart at either theme park or *CityWalk*.

The Quick Service Dining Plan can be redeemed at all food locations owned and operated by Universal Orlando in Universal Studios Florida (except 'Leaky Cauldron') and Islands of Adventure, and at select *CityWalk* locations including Hot Dog Hall of Fame and Bread Box.

In our opinion the quick service plan is not going to be a great purchase if you are looking for value for money, as you would really have to try hard to profit from this dining plan and you would need to eat the most expensive entrees on the menu. If, however, you simply want to have the whole day's meals paid for in advance then you may enjoy this option. If you are using one of the refillable drink options discussed later in this chapter you are guaranteed to lose money with the Quick Service Dining Plan as refill as so cheap.

Universal Dining Plan

Unlike the Quick Service Universal Dining Plan, the Universal Dining Plan is only available to guests who have booked a vacation package through Universal Parks & Resorts Vacation or an authorized reseller – this includes both on-site and off-site hotels. The Dining Plan cannot be purchased in the parks in any form.

The cost of the dining plan is $51.99 + tax for adults and $17.99 for children (Ages 3 to 9).

Each day purchased on the Dining Plan entitles you to:
1 Table Service meal - with Entree, Dining Plan Dessert and Non-alcoholic beverage.
1 Quick service meal - with Entree and Non-alcoholic beverage.
1 Snack - From food carts or quick service locations such as popcorn, ice cream or a frozen beverage.
1 Beverage - From food carts or quick service locations.

For those familiar with the Disney Dining Plan at Walt Disney World this is very similar in nature but there is one crucial difference: whereas at Disney you have to purchase a Dining plan for the entire stay, (e.g. At Disney an 8 day stay would mean you would have to purchase 8 days of dining plan), at Universal you only buy however many days' worth of credits you need. So it would be possible to purchase 3 days' worth of food during an 8-day stay. You must however purchase the plan for every member of your family aged over 2.

Furthermore, you do not need to use all your credits in 3 days, or even 3 consecutive days. For example with a 3 day dining package you would get 3 table service meal credits, 3 quick service meal credits, 3 snack credits and 3 beverage credits. With the Universal Dining Plan you could split these between several days throughout the entire duration of your stay. You could have a table service meal one day and a snack, and then two quick service meals another day - however you want to do it, the credits are available for your entire stay.

The Universal Dining Plan can be redeemed at most food locations owned and operated by Universal Orlando in Universal Studios Florida and Islands of Adventure, and at select *CityWalk* locations including Antojitos, Margaritaville and Red Oven Pizza Bakery. No on-site hotel restaurants are part of this dining plan.

Guests who purchase the Dining Plan must pick up their dining plan card with their credits to use the scheme. You will receive a voucher when you have booked your vacation to be exchanged in the theme parks or *CityWalk*. The voucher can be exchanged for a card at the Ticket Centre Desk at either theme park, Guest Services at either theme park or Dining Reservation Carts at either theme park or *CityWalk*. It can also be picked up at on-site hotels.

For an upcharge of $20 per adult or $7 per child you can use one of your credits for the Cinematic Spectacular Dining Experience at Lombard's Seafood Grille. You can also use one full service credit without an upcharge for the Superstar Character Breakfast at Cafe La Bamba.

Our opinion: The Dining Plan is still relatively new having only been unveiled in July 2013 and as such when compared with Disney's system the dining plan still has a few niggles to work out. Firstly, exchanging a voucher given at booking for a card is annoying and potentially time consuming. Secondly, eating locations in *CityWalk* are still limited on the plan - all the other restaurants are inside the theme parks, so you will need admission for the days you plan to eat with the plan. Annoyingly, no on-site hotel restaurants are included either.

Thirdly, each card is assigned its own credits and operates independently. As such a parent wanting to get four ice creams needs to have all cards with them and each ice cream would be processed separately. The credits are not grouped between cards like the Disney Dining Plan. As such it can potentially be a time consuming affair.

If, however, you like having all your meals pre-paid and have one less expense to worry about and like eating table service meals then this is the perfect plan for you. In addition, this plan does generally offer better value than the Quick Service dining plan, especially if you eat the most expensive items on the menus, meaning that you can end up saving money here.

Note: Gratuities are not included in the price of the Dining Plan.

List of all Universal Dining Plan locations:

Universal Studios Florida:
Finnegan's Bar and Grill - Table Service location.
Louie's Italian Restaurant - Quick Service location.
Richter's Burger Co. - Quick Service location.
Lombard's Seafood Grille - Table Service location.
San Francisco Pastry Company - Sandwiches and Pastries location.
Fast Food Boulevard - Quick Service location.
Mel's Drive In - Quick Service location.
Beverly Hills Boulangerie - Quick Service location.
Leaky Cauldron – Quick service location (buy only on the table service dining plan)

Islands of Adventure:
Confisco Grill and Backwater Bar - Table service location.
Croissant Moon Bakery - Quick service location.
Circus McGurks Cafe Stoo-pendous - Quick Service location.
Mythos Restaurant - Table Service location.
Fire Eater's Grill - Quick Service location.
Three Broomsticks - Quick Service location
The Burger Digs - Quick Service location.
Thunder Falls Terrace - Quick Service location.
Blondie's - Quick Service location.
Comic Strip Cafe - Quick Service location.
Captain America Diner - Quick Service location.
Cafe 4 - Quick Service location.

CityWalk:
Antojitos Authentic Mexican Food – Table service location.
Bob Marley – A Tribute to Freedom– Table service location.
Breadbox – Quick Service location.
Cold Stone Creamy – Quick service location. Dining Plan for selected snacks.
Cinnabon – Quick service location. Dining Plan for selected snacks.
Hot Dog Hall of Fame – Quick Service location.
Jimmy Buffet's Margaritaville – Table service location.
Menchie's Frozen Yogurt – Quick Service location.

NBA City – Table service location.
Pat O' Briens – Table service location.
Red Oven Pizza Bakery – Quick Service location.
Starbucks Coffee – Accepts Universal Dining Plan for selected snacks and beverages only.
Vivo Italian Kitchen – Table service location.

Refillable Cups, Coca Cola Freestyle and Popcorn Buckets

There are two different options for refillable drinks in the theme parks: the classic refillable cups and the coca cola freestyle refillable cups.

A refillable cup costs $8.99 plus tax. Once you have purchased the cup you are then eligible for discounted refills priced at 99 cents plus tax. The cups can be refilled virtually everywhere within the two theme parks that serves fountain drinks – that is pretty much every quick-service and full-service location, but not food carts. You can also have your cup refilled in *CityWalk*, but not at any of the on-site hotels. Once you have purchased one of these cups you can get unlimited 99-cent refills for life under the current policy. Note that refills are for fountain drinks only such as Coca Cola, Fanta and Sprite. You will not be able to get discounted refills on any specialty drinks such as Butterbeer or any specialty drinks from Simpsons' Fast Food Blvd. You can also get discounts on refills of tea, lemonade, and cider inside the Wizarding World of Harry Potter, and for slushies and ICEEs elsewhere at the parks.

Refillable popcorn buckets work in the same way as the refillable cups listed above - you pay $5.99 for the popcorn bucket and then refills are $1.29 cents plus tax each - there are four places at each theme park where your souvenir bucket can be refilled: just look for the big popcorn machines - these are usually outdoors. There are no popcorn refills at *CityWalk*, nor at any of the on-site hotels. Popcorn refills are also available for standard popcorn; flavored popcorn is not available at a discount and must be purchased at full price.

Finally there are the Coca Cola Freestyle machines which operate in a completely different manner to the two aforementioned schemed. Essentially you pay $11.99 plus tax for a Coca Cola Freestyle cup. You then visit any of the 8 Coca Cola Freestyle locations - 4 in each park (all in quick-service restaurants bar one in *Islands of Adventure*) and refill your cup for free for that day – there are also other Freestyle machines throughout the parks that are not inside quick service locations. The cup has an RFID chip and will only be activated for that day - so after that the cup will not work for free refills. There are over 100 different Coke drink mixes you can choose from at the machine, or you can stick to the plain old coke products – it is up to you. Making you wait ten minutes between refills with Coca Cola Freestyle discourages sharing. Additional days can be added at $5.99 a day. There are no Coke Freestyle stations at CityWalk or any of Universal's on-site hotels that can be used at this system.

Dining reservations:

Dining at Universal Orlando is varied - ranging from quick service meals to full-blown table service locations. When you want to sit down and have a meal in a busy theme park, you do not want to be kept waiting and you want to make sure there is a seat reserved for you. That is where dining reservations come in. Now, if you are thinking "What? I have to think about what I am going to be eating in 4, 5 or 12 months time?" then do not fret.

Unlike some of the other theme parks in the area (such as those operated by a mouse), at Universal you will not have trouble making dining reservations. There is no need to sit by your computer 180 days before you want your meal either. Instead, it is simple - browse online through the various restaurants and their menus and book your table whenever you want at no cost to you. With the exception of very busy seasons, you should be able to get a reservation for a restaurant even 4 or 5 days in advance for most places. If there is a specific place you want to eat we recommend you book your table as soon as possible, however we have frequently decided that we would like to eat a particular location and have known to get reservations on the very same day.

If you do want to book in advance, then the official Universal website is the place to go. You will need to visit https://www.universalorlando.com/Restaurants/50-Great-Restaurants.aspx.

Once you are on the website you will be able to look through the various restaurants, look at the menus and then click the links to book through OpenTable.com. We do not recommend going directly to the OpenTable website as it is very hard to navigate and find all the restaurants at the resort on one page.

Top 5 Table Service restaurants at Universal:

Universal has table service restaurants dotted across its theme parks, *CityWalk* and resort hotels so finding the best one can be a bit of a task. Luckily, we have rounded up those that you really should not miss out on below. Note that prices and entrees change all the time with seasons and chefs - those which we have listed were correct as of when we ate at the locations and should merely be taken as examples.

1. Mythos *(Islands of Adventure)* – Mythos is often rated the number one theme park restaurant in all of Orlando, let alone just Universal. Mythos is a pure delight to eat in, with its lavish interiors, exotic menu and, perhaps surprisingly, rather fair prices. Mythos will truly transport you to a different world. Entrees are priced between $1e and $20. The food ranges from sandwiches to Shortribs, Asian Salmon and Mahi Mahi. Note: Mythos is often only open for lunch.

2. Finnegan's Bar and Grill *(Universal Studios Florida)* – Finnegan's is always a fun place to dine in or to simply go in for a quick drink. Themed as an Irish Pub, there is a lot of fun to be had as well as some delightful treats. Entrees are priced between $10 and $22. The food ranges from sandwiches to Fish n' Chips, Beef Stew and Sirloin Steak.

3. Confisco Grille & Backwater bar *(Islands of Adventure)* - Located at in the *Port of Entry* park entrance area, Confisco Grille has a more traditional range of theme park food which may be better for families with younger children who are not quite ready to eat the Mahi Mahi at Mythos. It is also a more relaxed atmosphere. Entrees are priced between $9 and $18. You will find wood-oven pizzas, sandwiches, pasta and fajitas to name just a few of the items on the menu.

4. NBA City *(CityWalk)* - Many ignore this restaurant when walking past, perhaps discounting it as tacky because of its basketball theme. Do not be one of the people that makes that mistake; NBA City has some great food on offer and the portions are huge! The desserts in particular are to die for - try the Cinnamon Berries and the fried Cheesecake for an unforgettable end to a meal. Entrees are priced between $10 and $34. There is a wide selection of food on offer from chicken quesadillas to pizzas, jambalaya, shrimp, salmon, pasta, and much more.

5. Emeril's *(CityWalk)* - Emeril's is the most premium of the table service dining experiences we have listed here, with prices to match. With New Orleans-inspired dishes, you can enjoy seeing your food be prepared in the open kitchen. Alternatively, indulge and book yourself into the Chef's private tasting room with room for ten people. Entrees are priced between $12 and $18 for lunch, and $24 to $30 for dinner. You will find food ranging from a soup of the day to shrimps and grits, calamari, lasagna and the 18-oz ultimate rib-eye steak.

Top 5 Quick Service restaurants:

Sometimes you do not necessarily want to sit down and have a three-course meal. You may want to use the time that you would spend eating to watch a show, walk around the parks or ride your favorite attraction again - but that does not mean you want to compromise on taste, and you will not have to with the best quick service restaurants all being listed here in this handy section. Note that prices and entrees change all the time with seasons and chefs - those which we have listed were correct as of when we ate at the locations and should merely be taken as examples.

1. Three Broomsticks *(Islands of Adventure)* - Everything about this restaurant puts it top of the pile of quick service locations: the atmosphere, the food and its opening hours. Three Broomsticks is open for all three meals: breakfast, lunch and dinner and is the only restaurant inside *The Wizarding World of Harry Potter - Hogsmeade*. Entrees are priced between $8 and $15. Breakfast entrees include breakfasts from around the world: English, American and Continental Europe just to name a few. Lunch and dinner fare revolves around British dishes with some American classics available too. You will find Cornish pasties, fish & chips, shepherd's pie, as well as smoked turkey legs, rotisserie smoked chicken and spareribs.

2. Thunder Falls Terrace *(Islands of Adventure)* - This is another restaurant where the atmosphere really brings you into the story. Step foot into Thunder Falls and you are right in the middle of the world of Jurassic Park - and you get a spectacular view of the River Adventure ride splashdown from the wall of glass diving the restaurant and the Jurassic world outside. Entrees are priced between $9 and $16. You will find cheeseburgers on sale, as well as ribs, smoked turkey legs, wraps, as well as rotisserie chicken. The portion sizes are large at this restaurant. The rotisserie chicken has been extremely dry every time we have eaten there so we cannot recommend that particular item, but the ribs are much better!

3. Louie's Italian Restaurant *(Universal Studios Florida)* - As far as pizzas and pasta go for inside the theme parks, Louie's does it best. Outside the parks **Red Oven Pizza Bakery** does pizza even better (another way of getting a quick honorable mention in this section). Although there is not a huge variety of food on offer at Louie's and it is not particularly healthy, what it does do it does very well. Entrees are priced between $6 and $14. You can also order a full pizza pie to share for between $29 and $36. Food on offer includes spaghetti and meatballs, pizza and fettuccine alfredo. The meatballs are surprisingly good for a theme park quick service location, as are the pizzas.

4. Krusty Burger *(Universal Studios Florida)* - If you want the slimiest of burgers then this is *the* place to go. Designed to be exactly as "artery-clogging" as the burgers are in 'The Simpsons' cartoons, Krusty Burger will not win any awards for being exotic but this location hands down has the best-tasting burgers at Universal. Entrees are priced between $8 and $13 with fries included. As well as burgers, you will find barbecue rib sandwiches and hot dogs.

5. Croissant Moon Bakery *(Islands of Adventure)* - The food at the Croissant Moon Bakery genuinely is really great-tasting and far from your standard theme park fare. However, it does not make it any higher up on the list because the bakery is not somewhere where you would go for a full-blown lunch or dinner meal, but rather is where you might prefer to go for breakfast or a light snack. **Top Tip**: This location is not listed on the theme park map; you will find it in the *Port of Entry* area of the park. Entrees are priced between $2.50 and $10. This location serves continental breakfasts, sandwiches, Paninis and most importantly delicious cakes! If you fancy a branded coffee, this is the place to go too!

Honorable Mention: 6. Leaky Cauldron *(Universal Studios Florida)* – Strangely the dining plan counts this as a table service meal but it is priced for guests at quick services prices. This location has a great atmosphere inside, and like its other Wizarding World companion in this section, you can be sure to get some good British grub at this location including Banger's and Mash, cottage Pie, Toad in the Hole, Fish and Chips and much more. Entrees are priced at $9 to $20 here.

Butterbeer Top Tips:

Butterbeer is the Wizarding World's signature drink and can be found in regular ($3.99) or frozen ($4.99) flavors - we recommend the frozen variety. Souvenir mugs can be purchased for an upcharge of $9 – these are merely souvenir mugs and do not provide discounted refills on Butterbeer but do for most other drinks.

Top Tip 1: If you are thinking of getting a Butterbeer in Hogsmeade go to the *Hog's Head* to get it - the lines are usually much shorter than from the carts outside and it is a fantastic place to relax.

Top Tip 2: If you want a Butterbeer in Hogsmeade at the start of the day then you will want to get it from the cart by Hogwarts Castle and not the one in Hogsmeade village opposite Dragon Challenge. The lines will be much shorter.

Chapter 12
Tips, Savings and More:

Money saving tips:

Bring food from home - Universal allows you to bring your own food into the parks so why not do exactly that? Whether it is a bag of chocolates or a drink, you can purchase these items at a fraction of the price anywhere outside of Universal property. For drinks, why not put them in a cooling bag (hard-sided coolers are not allowed in the parks) and/or freeze them to be drunk throughout the day. Food should be fine to be kept in a backpack throughout the day.

Bring rain gear – There is a high likelihood that at some point during your Universal theme park adventure you will get wet - whether that is through one of the water rides or play areas, or whether you get caught in one of the famous Floridian thunderstorms. Either way we recommend you bring some sort of rain protection from home - either a raincoat, a poncho or even an umbrella (be aware of lightning and umbrellas though). This saves you 1) from purchasing these items in the theme parks at very inflated prices, and 2) buying new clothes when you get soaked to replace what you already have. Another tip: Those big human dryers outside the water rides that you can pay $5 to go into are not very effective – do not waste your money.

Buy tickets in advance - Whatever you do, do not buy tickets at the gate or you will waste time and pay more than you need to. As you are reading this guide, we can safely assume that you will be doing some planning before you go, so there is no excuse not to buy your tickets in advance. You can do this over the phone, online at www.universalorlando.com or through a third party - either way you will save at least $20 per multi-day ticket by not purchasing them at the gate. What's more, if you purchase these tickets through the official Universal website you will receive a coupon which you can exchange for a booklet with up to $150 in savings vouchers. In addition, certain countries will find that they can get special deals such as the UK where you can get a 14-day ticket for the price of a standard 2-day two-park ticket on the official Universal Orlando website.

You do not NEED an Express Pass - If you make sure to follow our touring plans you will be able to complete both Universal Parks in two days, so if you can spare two days then Express Pass simply is not needed: you can save up to $135 per person on Express Passes alone.

If you want Express Passes, then stay on-site - On site hotels are expensive but one little-known perk of staying on-site at a deluxe hotel is that you get unlimited Express Passes for everyone staying in the room. The best bit is that you will get Unlimited Express Passes for the entire duration of your stay including both check in and checkout days. One great way to make the most of this is to simply book a one-night stay at a Universal hotel. On your check-in day despite the fact your room will only be available from 3:00pm onwards you can actually check in at any time and leave your bags and receive your Express Passes – this means you can theoretically get there at 7:00am or 8:00am and check in. On your checkout day your Express Passes are valid until theme park closing, even after you check out. Note: Express Passes are not included in rooms at the Cabana Bay Beach Resort, only at the deluxe on-site hotels.

Stay off-site - If you do not want to pay the (quite frankly ludicrous) prices to stay at the on-site deluxe hotels, then stay off-site. There are hotels that are only a two to three minute drive away, or 10-minute walk to the parks that cost a fraction of that charged by Universal. Plus at the Universal hotels you will have to pay the $20 per night parking fee and the deluxe hotels require you to pay for use of the fitness suite, which you do not have to at many off-site locations.

Loyalty Cards - AAA members, American Express Card holders and UK-based AA members can all receive different discounts throughout the resort. The AAA/AA discount is usually of 10% at restaurants though be sure to ask for it any time you pay for anything.

Ride photos - Universal are pretty strict on you not being allowed to take photos of the park monitors showing your on-ride photos. As such we recommend that if you are planning on buying ride photos, you should purchase the Star Card that is explained elsewhere in this guide. It will pay for itself if you plan on buying just a few ride photos

Stay at a partner hotel - Stay at one of Universal's partner hotels and you will receive in-room coupons whether you have booked the room directly or not, and depending on who you booked it with you may get early park admission too.

Free lockers - Universal charges for lockers on water rides but not on any other rides. Would they know for example if you put your belongings in another ride's lockers which are free and then walked over to the water ride? Absolutely not. It is up to you to decide if you use this trick or not as it does involve walking back and forth. If you will be doing this, be prepared to do a lot of walking to save a few dollars. Also be prepared to look around for the ride with the longest wait times to store your belongings in - *Harry Potter and the Forbidden Journey* often has long wait times but also has a very crowded locker area – *Harry Potter and the Escape from Gringotts* is similar but with a less crowded locker area.

Get a *CityWalk* coupon book - This is a completely free coupon book offering savings all across *CityWalk*. You can get it from the small kiosk near the elevator between the two floors of *CityWalk*. You can also get dining information here. Vouchers from here are generally for food and not for merchandise, though the vouchers do vary.

Use the single rider lines - This is more of a time-saving tip than a money-saving one: if you do not mind riding separately from the rest of your party, take advantage of single rider lines - they will reduce your time in queue lines significantly meaning you can experience more things per day, and that means you may be able to cut a day off your time at Universal, saving yourself the entry and food price for that day.

How to spend less time queuing:

Park opening - Make sure you get to the theme park by the time it opens - ideally you should at the gate 30 minutes or more before opening. Remember it will take some time to park your car and get to the parks if you are doing this. Early morning is the quietest point of the day and in the first hour you can usually do two or three of the biggest rides, something that would take several hours during the day. The gates are also often opened early than advertised, particularly during busy periods.

Touring Plans – We have expertly crafted touring plans which tell you what order to do the attractions in, these are devised to let you see as much as possible whilst spending as little time as is possible in lines. Use them.

Parades and Fireworks - If you have a desire to get on rides and no desire to see parades or fireworks, then use the time the shows are on to visit the big rides, as crowds dwindle during these big events

Parades - As a follow up tip, do not ride attractions near the parade route immediately after the parade, they will be busier than usual.

The 59-minute rule - If Universal closes its parks at 9:00pm then that means that at that time the lines (not the rides) will be closed. Anyone in the queue line at park closing time will be allowed to ride, no matter how long the line is. This means that if you have one final ride to do and it is getting to park closing time make sure that you are in line before the park closes and you will still be able to ride. This rule may not apply is an attraction has an exceptionally long line which would cause it to keep running for hours after park closing – recently, notably, *Escape from Gringotts* has limited guest entry before the park officially closes.

Early Park Admission

How do you fancy being able to get into the theme parks before other guests? Benefit from much shorter queue lines and an emptier park with Universal's Early Park Admission.

During slower seasons of the year when there are fewer guests, Universal Orlando offers early entry to one theme park. At the time of writing the theme park which currently offers early entry every day is *Universal Studios Florida* and *Universal's Islands of Adventure*. This benefit is available to on-site hotel guests and guests who have booked a Universal Vacation Package for every day of their stay including their check-in and check-out days.

At *Universal Studios Florida* you will be able to access *The Wizarding World of Harry Potter: Diagon Alley* and its attractions, minus the Hogwarts Express which opens at the same time as *Islands of Adventure*.

Although at the time of writing early access to *Islands of Adventure* is not currently offered, Universal Orlando may offer this in the future. Speaking from past experience, you will usually be able to access *The Wizarding World of Harry Potter: Hogsmeade* including all attractions, and usually one attraction within *Seuss Landing* - most of the time this is *The Cat in the Hat*, but this is subject to change.

Early entry is offered every day of the year for those staying at on-site hotels. It is also offered with vacation packages booked through Universal whether staying on-site or not, as long as you have booked through Universal and purchased accommodation and park tickets together.

How do I get Early Park Admission?

For those staying at any on-site Universal hotel you must show your room key to gain early admission to the parks. If this is on your arrival date then make sure you check-in before Early Admission starts and then go over to the parks - when you check-in you will be given a room key; your room will not be ready but you will have Early Access to one or both parks. You may be sent a text message with your room number later on - if you do not receive it, simply stop by the front desk to get your room number.

For those with a Universal Vacation Package staying off-site you do not need to check in to your hotel room, simply go straight to the Will Call kiosks located by the entrance to each park - here you can enter your confirmation number given to you when booking to redeem your tickets with Early Park Admission. We advise you bring your "E-Travel Document" which was also given to you when you booked the package - this proves that you are entitled to this benefit in case there are any problems at the turnstiles.

Entry is one hour before regular park opening - meaning early entry is allowed from 8:00am most of the year (with the park opening for regular guests at 9:00am), and 7:00am during peak season.

Character Meet & Greets

Meeting characters can be one of the most enjoyable parts of a day in a theme park for many visitors – luckily, at Universal, there are many characters to meet. Usually the characters have little-to-no queues unlike those at Disney, which makes the experience even better.

At *Islands of Adventure* in *Marvel Superhero Island* you will usually find Captain America, Dr. Doom, The Green Goblin, Spiderman, Storm and Wolverine. They even make their appearances (and disappearances) on cool quad bikes most of the time. You can also meet the Seuss characters at *Seuss Landing* including Cat in the Hat, the Grinch, the Lorax and even Thing 1 and 2!

At *Universal Studios Florida* you will find the characters from the Simpsons including Bart, Homer, Marge and Sideshow Bob all in the new Simpsons mini-land, you will also see the Blues Brothers, the Men in Black, Shrek, Fiona and Donkey, Barney, SpongeBob, the Minions and Gru and the Transformers characters regularly around the park in their respective areas outside their attractions. There are also other characters that occasionally make appearances such as Scooby Doo and Shaggy, Lucy Ball, Woody Woodpecker and Marilyn Monroe.

You can find out what times a certain character will be out by looking at your park map which will have character times listed. Some characters will not be listed on the map such as Scooby Doo but will make periodic appearances in the parks' Character Zones - these are located near the turnstiles at *Universal Studios Florida*, and in the *Toon Lagoon* area at *Islands of Adventure*.

Operating Hours and Ride Closures

It is important to note that the Universal Orlando Resort is open 365 days a year - as such the operating hours of the parks vary according to demand. We strongly advise that you check these in advance of your visit.

This can be done about two months in advance at https://www.universalorlando.com/Resort-Information/Theme-Park-Hours.aspx. Busier times of the year such as school break mean longer operating hours, whereas not so busy periods mean the parks will shut earlier.

Ride refurbishments also happen throughout the year in order to keep rides operating safely and efficiently. As the Universal Orlando Resort does not close for several months on end to refurbish rides like some other theme parks, rides and attractions must close throughout the year in order to be renewed. Refurbishments tend to avoid the busier times of the year. Be sure to check in advance to avoid disappointment with ride closures though unfortunately these are only published a month or so in advance - these can be checked on the same page where the operating hours are posted.

Ride Height Requirements

Many attractions at the universal Orlando resort have height requirements meaning that not everyone in your party may be able to enjoy every attraction height requirements are put in place for the safety of all guests to ensure they fit in the ride vehicles correctly. You will need to be measured at the entrance to each ride by a ride operator if you may be close to the height limit – their word is final. This section helpfully lists all attractions (except those without height requirements) in ascending order of height. Next to each attraction name you will find USF or IOA denoting whether the attraction is in Universal Studios Florida or in Universal's Islands of Adventure.

- **E.T. Adventure (USF)** - 34 inches (0.87m)
- **Pteranodon Flyers (IOA)** - The minimum height is 36 inches (0.92m). Guests over 56 inches (1.43m) must be accompanied by someone under 36 inches (0.92m) to ride.
- **Woody Woodpecker's Nuthouse Coaster (USF)** - 36 inches (0.92m)
- **Flight of the Hippogriff (IOA)** – 36 inches (0.92m)
- **The Cat in the Hat (IOA)** – 36 inches (0.92m) minimum to ride with an adult, or 48 inches (1.22m) to ride alone
- **The Amazing Adventures of Spider-Man (IOA)** – 40 inches (1.02m)
- **Despicable Me: Minion Mayhem (USF)** - 40 inches (1.02m)
- **TRANSFORMERS: The Ride-3D (USF)** - 40 inches (1.02m)
- **The Simpsons Ride (USF)** – 40 inches (1.02m)
- **The High in the Sky Seuss Trolley Train Ride (IOA)** – 40 inches (1.02m) minimum to ride accompanied by an adult, or 48 inches (1.22m) to ride alone
- **MEN IN BLACK: Alien Attack (USF)** - 42 inches (1.07m)
- **Popeye & Bluto's Bilge-Rat Barges (IOA)** - 42 inches (1.07m)
- **Jurassic Park River Adventure (IOA)** - 42 inches (1.07m)
- **Harry Potter and the Escape from Gringotts (USF)** – 42 inches (1.07m)
- **Dudley Do-Right Ripsaw Falls (IOA)** – 44 inches (1.12m)

- **Storm Force Accelatron** - An adult must accompany those under 48 inches (1.22m)
- **Revenge of the Mummy (USF)** - 48 inches (1.22m)
- **One Fish, Two Fish, Red Fish, Blue Fish (IOA)** – Children under 48 inches (1.22m) must ride with an adult
- **Harry Potter and the Forbidden Journey (IOA)** – 48 inches (1.22m)
- **Hollywood Rip Ride Rockit (USF)** - Minimum 51 inches (1.29m) / Maximum 79 inches (2.00m)
- **Doctor Doom's Fearfall (IOA)** - **52 inches (1.32m)**
- **Dragon Challenge (IOA)** – 54 inches (1.37m)
- **The Incredible Hulk Coaster (IOA)** – 54 inches (1.37m)

Chapter 13
Comparing Universal Orlando and Walt Disney World

Universal Orlando cannot be studied in a vacuum - it is not the only theme park in Orlando. Far from it; if it were not for the other big competitor in the district, Universal most likely would not even have a theme park in Florida. We are of course referring to the Walt Disney World Resort - the world's most visited tourist destination. There is no doubt that one day Universal would like to greet just as many guests as Disney does.

The two resorts - Universal Orlando and Walt Disney World - can be compared. There are many similarities and many differences so if you have visited one and not the other this section should be able to provide you with some sort of insight into what to expect. We hope this will help you be more prepared for your Universal Orlando experience.

Resort size - Universal is but a needle in a haystack in comparison to Disney World. Disney world covers 47 square miles, an area twice the size of Manhattan. Universal Orlando in comparison is about 1 square mile in size. Yes, it is a much smaller resort but be aware there are both advantages and disadvantages to this.

Walt Disney World hosts four theme parks, two water parks, golf and mini-golf courses, almost thirty resort hotels, dozens of miles of roads, a speedway, lakes, a shopping district and much, much more. It is also important to note that Disney has only developed one third of its 47 square miles. Even so, Disney's currently developed property real estate is about 15 times larger than Universal's. Universal has two theme parks, four resort hotels (with a fifth one coming soon) and a shopping district which is significantly smaller than Disney's.

This means that Disney World naturally has more things to do; it has the scope to create larger developments - just Animal Kingdom Park alone at Walt Disney World is about 580 acres in size for example. The whole of Universal's land can fit in Animal Kingdom and its parking lot. This does not mean that Universal has not done a lot with the land it has though, in many ways it is far more efficient with the space it has.

The sheer size of the resort does also mean that it can take an eternity to get anywhere at Walt Disney World - you may be staying at an on-site hotel but it can easily be a 20-minute bus journey to the theme parks. Whereas, at Universal you are much closer to the action and can catch a boat to the theme parks from most hotels in a matter or minutes or even walk from all hotels.

Lastly, it is important to note that because of its size you are much more likely to spend one, two or even three weeks at Walt Disney World, whereas you would struggle to fill more than four days at Universal Orlando.

Planning - A vacation/holiday to Walt Disney World cannot be done without A LOT of planning - you need to research which ticket type you want, which of the resort hotels you want to stay at (and there are a lot to choose from), which theme park you want to visit on which day and potentially have to book your restaurants 180 days before you even step foot on Disney property. You then best have a strategy about which rides to do when, know the ins and outs of the Fastpass+ system and know what times the characters meet and greet to make the most of your time – you will even need to make ride and show reservations 30 to 60 days in advance to get the most out of your ticket price.

A Universal Orlando vacation/short break *does* require some planning, we will not lie to you. We are sure you know that because you have purchased this guide. It does, however, not require anywhere near the degree of planning that a Walt Disney World vacation does. You can take it more at your own pace. There are only four on-site hotels to choose from which greatly reduces the time looking at those, though there are many nearby off-site hotels to consider. Ticket options are simpler: you simply decide how many days and then whether you want to park-hop or not. Restaurants can be booked much closer to the day, sometimes on the day itself - sometimes a week or so in advance, but definitely not 180 days out like at Disney.

As far as having a strategy of what rides and experiences you do when, we recommend that you have this at all theme parks - Universal included. You will not however need to make ride reservations for Universal like you do at Disney, because this is (thankfully) simply not possible. So, there is still some planning to do for a Universal Orlando vacation but it is a lot less than at Walt Disney World.

Off-Season - We all know that school breaks are going to be busy, the kids are out of school and parents want them to have fun so the theme parks are naturally quite busy. What about out of season? Like September during school time, or February. At Walt Disney World you can expect some crowds year round – there are much quieter days than others but there is never going to be a day at Disney World you can walk into EPCOT and walk onto Soarin' within 5 minutes - this is never going to happen.

This is different at Universal; there are still lots of times of the year in off-season where every ride is a walk-on or near walk-on - times when you can experience *Harry Potter and the Forbidden Journey* in a matter or minutes instead of hours! Off-season still exists at Universal. We think this may have a lot to do with the target demographic of Universal with older teens likely being in school for longer, whereas young kids are often not in school and can visit Disney year-round. At the same time Disney also generally appeals more to the older, retired population than Universal so it attracts them year-round too.

Having said this, if Universal Orlando continues to soar in popularity as it has done in recent years (in 2013 for example the Universal Orlando theme parks welcomed 7.2% - or 1 million - more guests than they did the year prior), it is very possible that the same situation will exist at universal Orlando particularly as the parks have a very limited number of attractions.

Character meet and greets - A small note, albeit related to 'planning' earlier on. At Walt Disney World you have to plan what characters to meet and when, at Universal its more spontaneous and you should never have to wait in more than a 5 or 10-minute queue. Compare that to a 180-minute wait for the princesses in Disney's *Magic Kingdom* and you can see the difference.

Hotel accommodation - We touched on this briefly earlier on in the 'resort size' section. Hotels on-site at Universal Orlando are physically much closer to the parks than those at Walt Disney World. However, there are a lot fewer choices and the three 'deluxe' hotels are expensive, though Cabana Bay offers a more reasonable value-moderate pricing range. The flip side is that there are off-site hotels located a 2-minute drive away or a 15-minute walk, unlike at Walt Disney World where offsite hotels are a considerable distance away.

Not locked in at Universal - This is related to our previous point. You can actually walk off-site at Universal Orlando and be at a Walgreens within 15 minutes. If you want to make the effort you can go and eat outside of the Universal resort and make significant savings on the price of food, as well as the price of accommodation. This is simply not possible at Walt Disney World without a car and more time.

Innovative attractions at Universal - This one will be controversial from the view of many Disney aficionados but in our opinion Universal is developing many more innovative and revolutionary experiences that Disney is simply missing out on. Yes, Walt Disney World has some incredible revolutionary experiences of its own - *Test Track, Soarin', Mickey's Philharmagic, Kilimanjaro Safaris, Rock n Rollercoaster*, and the *Tower of Terror* to name but a few.

However, in our opinion in the same timespan Universal has blown Disney out of the water - Universal Orlando only opened in 1990 and the resort is dotted with innovative experiences - *The Incredible Hulk Coaster* wins coaster awards year after year, the same can be said for *The Amazing Adventures of Spider-Man*. There is *Rip Ride Rockit, Harry Potter and the Forbidden Journey, Harry Potter and the Escape from Gringotts, Hogwarts Express, The Simpsons Ride, Jaws (now gone), Dueling Dragons, Jurassic Park River Adventure* and many more incredible experiences. The attractions opened at Universal Orlando over the past few years have been immense. The last big revolution for Disney in our opinion was *Expedition Everest* in 2006. We would not count the additions in *New Fantasyland* as major attractions with perhaps the exception of *Enchanted Tales with Belle*.

Furthermore, guests at the Universal Orlando resort can expect new attractions every year for the foreseeable future as well as an expansion of the whole resort overall – we may even see a new theme park in the next 5 to 10 years.

Lockers - Just a small quirk but it is something to get used to and be aware of. Whereas at Walt Disney World you can take your belongings onto every ride and keep them at your feet or in your pockets, at Universal you must leave them in (free) lockers whilst you are riding. This can be an annoying process though admittedly it is safer for guests.

Friendliness - Although Universal Orlando has recently improved on the friendliness of Team Members; their employees are still nothing like Disney's. Disney's Cast Members are empowered to "make magical moments" to improve anyone's vacation the way Universal employees just are not. Disney employees seem happier, and have "courtesy" employed as one of 4 key values that must always be followed. At Disney parks the only reason the courtesy of an employee to be compromised would be in a safety-critical situation, otherwise the Cast Members cannot do enough for you - most will go above and beyond, and provide exceptional customer service. Universal Orlando on the other hand provides good service for the most part and most of the Team Members are great but it seems that all too often during a visit these employees have been overshadowed by those who are unhelpful or simply downright rude. Your mileage may vary here.

Live entertainment – You would think for a company that is celebrating 100 years of movies Universal would know how to put on a good show or two. They do - just not at Universal Orlando. The *Universal Studios Hollywood* theme park in California is filled with great shows yet sadly none have made their way across to Orlando. Shows like *SindBad*, *Beetlejuice* and even *Fear Factor* are old and aging badly. In comparison shows like *Dream Along with Mickey*, *Find Nemo the Musical* and *The Festival of the Lion King* are incredible and innovative.

Unfortunately it is much the same with parades and fireworks - although better than many other theme parks, Universal's offering simply are nowhere near as good as any of Disney's parades or nighttime shows.

FASTPASS+ vs. Express Pass - At Walt Disney World your park ticket enables you access to make free Fastpass+ reservations, which let you skip the regular line by giving you a certain time to ride. You can make these in advance or on the day of your visit itself – if made in advance it is a good way of guaranteeing that you will do at least a certain number of attractions. It is a bit of a complicated system to understand but guidebooks like *The Independent Guide to Walt Disney World 2015* go through the whole process in detail.

Express Pass at Universal allows you instant entry to almost all attractions for a fee – this fee can be very high and up to $135 per person per day.

Leaving aside the fact that Disney's Fastpass+ is obviously a much better value as it is free, Universal's Express Pass because of its paid nature works as a much better system to get on rides - there is rarely more than a 10 minute wait, you do not make reservations in advance, there is no complicated system to understand, less people use it and it is available for almost every single attraction.

Target Audience - This is one of the most striking differences between the two resorts. Universal Orlando caters more towards teenagers and adults; Walt Disney World targets families and younger kids more.

With the exception of rides like *Rock N Rollercoaster, Tower of Terror, Expedition Everest, Mission: SPACE* and possibly *Test Track*, there are few things that will get the adrenaline rushing for teenagers at the Walt Disney World resort. Disney caters more towards the families with experiences such as *Soarin', Big Thunder Mountain, Kilimanjaro Safaris* and character experiences uniting the whole family. At the same time the really small ones can enjoy classics such as *Peter Pan's Flight* and *it's a small world*.

Universal Orlando is very different. There are a few things for the smaller ones, which we have covered in more detail elsewhere in this guide, but for the most part it is high intensity thrills that people come to Universal for as well as big family adventures - *The Incredible Hulk Coaster*, *Dueling Dragons*, *Hollywood Rip Ride Rockit* and *Dr. Doom's Fear Fall* to name but a few.

The family experiences on offer are generally more adult-oriented too: *Harry Potter and the Forbidden Journey* and *Harry Potter and the Escape from Gringotts* are rougher than most rides at Disney, and the same can be said for *The Amazing Adventures of Spider-Man*, *The Simpsons* and *Transformers: The Ride*. Even an attraction like *Twister* manages to feel more intense than most things run by the mouse. Although there are some attractions for the smaller members of the family such as *Barney*, these are few and far between at Universal Orlando.

Less strollers – This is another minor consideration, but the fact that more visitors to the park are adults means that one advantage is that you do not have to swim through a sea of strollers or pushchairs to get to your favorite attraction. Strollers and small children are well accepted throughout the parks but there are simply less of them.

Dining - Food at Universal Orlando is generally cheaper than at Walt Disney World. There is nowhere near as much variety at Universal as there is at Disney though; you will pretty much have to stick to standard theme park food. The biggest difference in our opinion however is the quality and taste; whilst food at the Disney parks is not gourmet by any standard in general it is much, much better than Universal Orlando's offerings.

Water Rides – You have ridden *Splash Mountain* at the *Magic Kingdom* in Disney World and you came out a little bit wet, having received a big of a spray to the face. This is nothing! Go on a water ride at Universal and you will not be coming out having been sprayed or splashed, you will come out drenched. Universal really does like to get you wet on these rides, and Universal's Islands of Adventure is the perfect place to do this with three major water attractions.

Resort transportation - We touched on this briefly before but due to the size of Disney's property there are various ways of getting to and from the theme parks to your hotel, all depending on where it is located. There are ferryboats, buses and monorails and journey times to the theme parks can be a few minutes to 25 minutes or more, but you may also require several transfers for certain trips. You can also walk between some limited areas of the Walt Disney World resort. Everyone can use the resort transportation for free.

Universal Orlando also allows everyone to use its resort transportation for free, which is made up of a fleet of ferryboats, which take you to and from the parks, *CityWalk* and the deluxe on-site hotels. The ferryboat journey should not take more than 10 minutes, or you can simply walk to the theme parks from all the on-site hotels (deluxe or not). You can walk across the entire resort at Universal Orlando; this is impossible to do at Disney, as they do not provide the means to do this with many areas not allowing pedestrian traffic. There are also complimentary shuttle buses available from all the on-site hotels to the parks at Universal Orlando.

Nightlife - As far as nightlife is concerned, Universal Orlando hands-down beats Walt Disney World. Universal has a much wider variety of clubs and bars and is truly considered a party scene. Disney does not do badly with some bars and a club, but it is just nowhere near the scale of Universal's offerings. Both resorts host a large-scale nighttime paid admission show – Blue Man at Universal, and Cirque du Soleil at Disney World.

Special events - Both Universal and Disney know that to keep people coming all year-round to the resort the parks need to diversify - this does not simply mean adding new attractions, but also different offerings year-round. As far as Halloween is concerned, Universal Orlando offers a much scarier portrayal of the season with *Halloween Horror Nights*, Disney goes for a "not so scary" approach. Christmas, however, is much bigger at Disney than at Universal with all four of the theme parks celebrating it in one way or another through unique shows, decorations, lighting ceremonies and even stories from around the world at EPCOT. Universal celebrates Mardi Gras and holds concerts. Disney holds concerts too and celebrates the Flower and Garden festival and the Food and Wine festivals too. Both resorts of course celebrate the New Year in style.

Chapter 14
Seasonal Events:

Universal offers something different all year round. Whether it is live entertainment, horror mazes or Holiday cheer, the Universal Orlando resort has it all covered. This section covers all of the seasonal events that happen throughout the year.

Christmas and Holidays 2014

December 2014
There is a surprising amount on offer during the Holiday season at Universal Orlando.
The 2014 holiday season runs from December 6th 2014 to January 3rd 2015.

At *Universal Studios Florida* watch as the Macy's Holiday Parade rolls through the streets with floats taken from the world-famous full-scale Thanksgiving Day Parade in New York City- this even runs every evening throughout the holiday season. Or celebrate the holiday season with the tree lighting ceremony!

You will also find live band "Mannheim steamroller" - the biggest selling Christmas band of all time - rocking the stage with live performances on 6th, 7th, 13th, 14th, 20th and 21st December 2014 – each performance will begin at 6:00pm and run for approximately one hour. In addition, Barney's *"A Day in the Park with Barney"* show gets a Christmas twist and runs multiple times each day, as does *The Blue's Brothers (Holiday) Show*.

At *Islands of Adventure* the fun continues. Watch the fantastic "*Grichmas Who-liday Spectacular*" - a 30-minute live-show with great music and starring The Grinch himself, telling you how the Grinch stole Christmas. If you fancy something to eat then why not meet the Dr Seuss characters at the holiday-season-only Character Breakfast with Grinch and Friends - reservations are required for this one. Finally, you can actually meet The Grinch - play, laugh and get some greet photos too!

Unfortunately, there are no meet and greets with Santa Claus at either park throughout the Holiday season - a bit of a missed opportunity if you ask us.

For the transition into the New Year head over to *CityWalk* and party the night away with live performances and a midnight champagne toast! A New Year's Eve party including club admission and unlimited gourmet cuisine will run with pricing from $100 to $120 plus tax.

A the time of writing, the 2015 holiday season is almost a year away and it is difficult to predict exactly what will be taking place at the time. However, Universal Orlando has been pretty consistent with its Holiday season over the years and we would expect all the above events to take place as they did in 2014.

A Celebration of Harry Potter 2015

January 30th 2015 to February 1st 2015

The 'Celebration of Harry Potter' event first ran at Universal Orlando in 2014 and proved such a success that it is returning in early 2015 for three full days of Wizarding fun. During the event you can see talent from the Harry Potter films, learn the proper way to wield a wand, tour props and set pieces from the films, see what Hogwarts house the Sorting Hat chooses for you, and much more. Most of the parts of this three day event are included in park admission and carry no additional charge. Full details are still not available at the time of writing but this is what we know so far. It is three magical days no Harry Potter fan will want to miss.

Film stars and autographs:
Several Harry Potter film stars will be present throughout the event, including to sign autographs. Park guests can expect to see:
- Michael Gambon (Albus Dumbledore)
- Robbie Coltrane (Rubeus Hagrid)
- Evanna Lynch (Luna Lovegood)
- James Phelps (Fred Weasley)
- Oliver Phelps (George Weasley)

A Celebration of Harry Potter Expo:
Make your way through interactive displays in this unique collection of Harry Potter themed props, movie sets, artwork and more. This year, Universal Orlando will welcome back Harry Potter: The Exhibition, Warner Bros. Studio Tour London, MinaLima, Pottermore.com, Scholastic, and Warner Bros. as part of the A Celebration of Harry Potter Expo.

- **The Sorting Hat Experience** – Are you a Gryffindor, or a Slytherin? A Hufflepuff? Perhaps a Ravenclaw? At the beginning of each school year the Sorting Hat sorts new Hogwarts students into their houses, and you'll have the opportunity to get sorted in a Hogwarts-inspired setting. Sponsored by Harry Potter: The Exhibition.
- **Warner Bros. Studio Tour London - The Making of Harry Potter** – Based at the production home of the Harry Potter film series, Warner Bros. Studio Tour London gives you the chance to step onto the actual sets used during

filming. For one time only, the Studio Tour is offering A Celebration of Harry Potter visitors the chance to pose for a photo in a recreation of the iconic Great Hall.

- **MinaLima** – Graphic designers Miraphora Mina and Eduardo Lima worked for ten years on the Harry Potter films, creating countless pieces of unforgettable artwork, some of which will be on display, including the Marauder's Map, Daily Prophet, and Hogwarts school books. Exclusive to A Celebration of Harry Potter, they will be launching their brand-new range of Harry Potter stationery, featuring the original film graphic artwork. Limited edition prints based on the original prop designs will also be exhibited.
- **Pottermore from J.K. Rowling** – Show your Hogwarts house colors and celebrate your pride with Pottermore from J.K. Rowling. For the millions of fans who have participated in our exclusive Sorting Hat quiz devised by J.K. Rowling herself, here's an amazing chance to take part in Pottermore's Proudest House Contest. Also, relive the excitement of a year in Pottermore and get an exclusive chance to have your say on what is to come.
- **Scholastic** – Celebrate Harry Potter and share your message about what Harry Potter means to you. Meet award-winning illustrator Kazu Kibuishi, who reimagined the Harry Potter book covers and will be signing posters on Saturday, January 31st. Be sure to enter our daily raffles for a chance to win a box set of all seven Harry Potter books and come by all weekend for a collectible Harry Potter giveaway!
- **Warner Bros.** – Do you have what it takes to defend yourself against a Dementor or soar above Hogwarts castle on Buckbeak? Step into some of your favorite scenes with this magical photo experience while surrounded by authentic movie props from the Harry Potter films.

Discussions & Demonstrations

- **Behind the Scenes: Harry Potter Film Talent Discussion** – Enjoy a fascinating and interactive question and answer session featuring some of your favorite actors from the Harry

Potter films. Discover what it was like to work on one of the most successful film franchises in history.

- **Duelling Demonstration & Wand Masterclass with Paul Harris** – Pick up your wand and take part in a live duelling masterclass, hosted by Warner Bros. Studio Tour London, featuring the world's only Wand Combat choreographer, Paul Harris. Paul choreographed the epic battle scenes in *Harry Potter and the Order of the Phoenix* and will be on hand to teach you the technique behind wielding a wand – with the help of a very special guest!

- **Creating The Wizarding World of Harry Potter** – Alan Gilmore, Art Director for the Harry Potter films, will explain how he and his team brought the world of Harry Potter to life from the fiction to the films, and eventually The Wizarding World of Harry Potter at Universal Orlando Resort. In addition, hear firsthand from Universal Orlando's Entertainment team how live shows in both Hogsmeade and Diagon Alley were created, as well as some of the hidden "secrets" and innovative interactive elements contained within The Wizarding World of Harry Potter.

- **Graphic Design for the Harry Potter Films with MinaLima** – Miraphora Mina and Eduardo Lima, from the graphic design studio MinaLima, will share insights into their role as Graphic Prop Designers, and how their paths crossed at the WB film studios to work for ten years on the Harry Potter movies. They will discuss and show some of the iconic props they created for the Harry Potter films, including the Marauder's Map, the *Daily Prophet* and *The Quibbler*, amongst others. Still immersed in all things Harry Potter, they will also talk about their recent involvement in The Wizarding World of Harry Potter - Diagon Alley, for which they designed all the street and store graphics.

- **Illustration of Harry Potter with Kazu Kibuishi** – Award-winning illustrator Kazu Kibuishi, who reimagined the Harry Potter book covers from Scholastic, will be demonstrating how to draw some of your favorite Harry Potter characters live on-stage in this interactive panel for all ages.

Demonstrations For The Younger Fans (Recommended for Ages 12 and Under)

- **Duelling Demonstration & Wand Masterclass with Paul Harris - Kids' Version** – Similar to the all ages version of the demonstration yet geared for a younger audience, ages 12 and under will learn proper wand duelling and usage from the world's only Wand Combat Choreographer, Paul Harris. Paul choreographed the epic battle scenes in *Harry Potter and the Order of the Phoenix* and will show exciting wand techniques. Presented by Warner Bros. Studio Tour London – The Making of Harry Potter, this demonstration will include a special reserved section just for kids.
- **Dance Like a Beauxbatons & Battle Like a Durmstrang** – If your younger Harry Potter fans are entranced by the dances performed by Beauxbatons and Durmstrang students in the Harry Potter films, they will love this demonstration. A Universal Orlando choreographer, working with Beauxbatons and Durmstrang students who perform here at The Wizarding World of Harry Potter, will explain the movements and techniques behind the mesmerizing dance routines.
- **Harry Potter Film Trivia** – How well do your children (or you) know the Harry Potter films? Test your knowledge during this fun audience-interaction game inviting younger fans to shout out the answers to film-specific questions. Perhaps a Harry Potter film marathon is in order before trying your luck?

Mardi Gras 2015

Select nights from February 7th 2015 to April 18th 2015.
Celebrate New Orleans with Universal's Mardi Gras celebrations running from February to April 2015 on select nights. Entry is included in your regular park admission.

Details for the 2015 edition of the season were not available at the time of publication. The following information is provided as a reference point and dates from the 2014 event.

Live concerts are the name of the game with the *Music Plaza stage* hosting live acts on select nights.

All concerts begin at 8:00pm or 8:30pm unless otherwise stated.

The line up for 2014 was:
Daughtry – February 8th
Barenaked Ladies – February 15th
Thomas Rhett – February 16th
Collective Soul – March 1st
Prince Royle – March 8th
Cody Simpson – March 14th
Foreigner – March 15th
A Great Big World – March 21st
Gavin DeGraw – March 22nd
Kelly Rowland – March 28th
Weezer – March 29th
Skillet – April 5th
Lynyrd Skynyryd – April 12th
Kool & The Gang – April 19th
Nelly – May 3rd
The Wanted – May 10th
The Roots – May 17th
Cher Lloyd – May 24th
Huey Lewis & The News – May 31st
Robin Thicke – June 7th

There is no seating area; it is all general standing room. For the best view of the concert you will need to skip the Mardi Gras Parade altogether or watch it from as close to the Music Plaza stage area as possible.

The highlight of the day for many is the Mardi Gras Parade with colorful floats and incredible music - be prepared for the traditional throwing of the beads from the floats for you to catch.

The French Quarter Courtyard area offers live New Orleans-style music and many stalls with local cuisine including jambalaya and gumbo. It opens at 4:00pm and closes at the concert start time.

A one-day after 5:00pm ticket is available to Florida residents only for $69.99 plus tax in advance (Call 407-224-7840) or $94.99 plus tax at the gate. These prices are for 2014 and may increase for the 2015 Mardi Gras event.

After the parks are shut head to the CityWalk bars and clubs for more New Orleans-inspired fun.

Top Tip 1: Note that when the parade starts the regular shows and attractions at the park will stop operating for the day.

Top Tip 2: Annual Pass-holders will be pleased to hear that there is a special parade viewing area reserved just for them.

Top Tip 3: The Power Pass has many black out dates but as a special bonus during Mardi Gras nights, Power Pass holders may enter on blackout dates after 5:00pm – making it perfect to get to see concerts at no extra cost. It is unclear whether this offer from 2014 will return in 2015.

Top Tip 4: For the little ones in the family, the *Little Jester's parade viewing area* is reserved just for them and their families! This parade viewing area opens up one hour before the parade begins and is located next to the Terminator 2: 3-D show.

Important Note: The Universal Cinematic Spectacular did not take place on Mardi Gras nights in 2014. It is unclear whether it will take place in 2015.

Grad Bash 2015

April and May 2015

Universal's *Grad Bash* is when High School Seniors get to celebrate their graduation in style.

The event runs from 7:00pm to 2:00am on April 17th, 24h and 25th, and May 1st and 2nd May 2015. Tickets also allow entry into one of two pre-parties: *CityWalk* (5:00pm-8:00pm), or *Universal Studios Florida* (5:00pm-7:00pm). Both pre-parties include a buffet dinner and entertainment.

During the *Grad Bash* night itself there are live concerts (including Trey Songz in 2015), karaoke sessions, dance parties, street entertainment and of course the chance to experience some thrilling attractions. A dress code is enforced during the event.

Some of the attractions operating during Grad Bash include both sides of the Wizarding World of Harry Potter, TRANSFORMERS: The Ride–3D, Despicable Me Minion Mayhem, The Amazing Adventures of Spider-Man, The Incredible Hulk Coaster and more attractions. That means that Grad Night guests get access to both theme parks!

More information can be obtained be emailing GradBash@UniversalOrlando.com or over the phone on 1-800-YOUTH15. Although ticket prices vary from school to school expect to pay around the $120 mark.

Gradventure 2015

May 2015

Gradventure is the opportunity for middle school kids to celebrate their graduation in style. With both theme parks open for the event, it is an experience unlikely any other in the world. Visitors can ride world-class rides and enjoy private theme park admission.

The event runs from 7:00pm to midnight on May 8th and May 15th 2015. At the *Gradventure* night itself there are Live DJs in attendance, Karaoke sessions, dance parties, street entertainment and of course the chance to experience some thrilling attractions.

Some of the attractions operating during Gradventure include both sides of the Wizarding World of Harry Potter and the Hogwarts Express, TRANSFORMERS: The Ride–3D, Despicable Me Minion Mayhem, The Amazing Adventures of Spider-Man, The Incredible Hulk Coaster and more attractions. That means that Grad Night guests get access to both theme parks!

More information can be obtained be emailing Gradventure@UniversalOrlando.com or over the phone on 1-800-YOUTH15. Although ticket prices vary from school to school expect to pay around the $75 mark.

Summer Concert Series 2015

Important Note: Before reading this information about the Summer Concert Series, be advised that the event did *not* take place in 2014. This was due to Diagon Alley opening last summer with Universal knowing it will not need to spend money on acts to draw in large crowds. There is no confirmation as to whether this event will return in 2015. The information below is for reference purposes only and relates to the 2013 event:

The *Summer Concert series* is an opportunity to check out some big acts in the park whilst getting some ride time in too. The *Universal Music Plaza* stage area near *Rip Ride Rockit* has bands playing on select dates throughout June and the beginning of July. There is no extra charge to listen to the live music and there can sometimes be some pretty big bands - all you need is your regular park admission ticket to get in. There is no seating area for the concert; it is all standing room.

Crowds do get very big for the *Summer Concert* nights and therefore attraction wait times can also be significantly longer than they otherwise would be.

If you do not want day admission to the theme park, a concert ticket can be purchased for $69.99 (as of 2013) - this allows you into the park from 7:00pm until park closing. Once inside you can either watch the concert or experience the attractions or a combination of both. Do note, that if you are going to be purchasing this ticket option that arriving at 7:00pm will *not* get you front row standing room for the concerts.

For reference, in 2013 all the concerts began at 8:00pm and were on Saturdays. This is subject to change in 2015 if the event runs. In 2013, there were several bands and artists on offer: NE-YO, Big Time Rush, Gavin DeGraw, 'Earth, Wind & Fire', Adam Lambert and Kip Moore. Expected the full line up to be announced in early May 2015 if the event does indeed run.

Rock the Universe 2015

September 2015
Billed as "Florida's Biggest Christian Music Festival", *Rock the Universe* is two days over a weekend where you can learn about the Christian faith and worship, all with Christian rock music of course. Select attractions also operate during the events.

There is also a free Sunday Morning Worship Service led by a guest speaker for those who hold *Rock the Universe* tickets. Reservations are required. Specific details have not yet been announced for the 2015 edition of the event, so the information below pertains to the 2014 edition of the event.

Rock the Universe is a separate ticketed event and guests must pay to access the event, even if they have a ticket for that day – it operates outside of regular park hours. 2014 entry tickets were priced at $57.99 for one night of the event, or $95.99 for both nights of the event. For $120.99 guests could enjoy both nights of the event plus admission to the park for three full days doing one park per day, or for $160.99 guests could enjoy both nights of the event plus admission to the park for three full days with park-to-park access for the whole weekend. Tickets allow access to *Universal Studios Florida* between 4:00pm and 1:00am. Overall, these tickets offer fantastic value for money.

The line-up for **Friday**, 5th September 2014 was: Third Day, Newsboys, Jeremy Camp, Kari Jobe, Soulfire Revolution, Rend Collective, About A Mile, and Veridia.

The line-up for **Saturday**, 6th September 2014 was: Switchfoot, tobyMac, Lecrae, Red, Family Force Five, Andy Mineo, Tedashii, and Love And The Outcome.

As well as the main stage, the Coca-Cola FanZone featured more live music in 2014, as well as band autograph sessions, karaoke, and more. The FanZone ran throughout both days of the event. The following acts appeared in the FanZone: Rapture Ruckus, Manafest, 7eventh Time Down and All Things Now.

Select attractions will also operate during the Rock the Universe 2015 event. In 2014 these attractions included TRANSFORMERS: The Ride-3D, Hollywood Rip Ride Rockit, Revenge of the Mummy, MEN IN BLACK Alien Attack, and The Simpsons Ride. Diagon Alley was closed throughout the 2014 event, and it is unclear whether it will open for the 2015 event.

On Saturday night guests can enjoy the Candelighting Ceremony, followed by a Sunday morning worship service the next day.

Top Tip: A one night Express Pass in 2014 could be purchased for $16 for one use per participating attraction or $25 for unlimited uses at participating attractions. These are a real bargain in our opinion, maybe because most people do not attend the event for the rides! Either way you can guarantee almost immediate access to your favorite rides for a small cost. We shall see if this returns in 2015.

Details about Rock the Universe 2015 should be available at some time in April 2015.

Halloween Horror Nights 2015

Select nights from September to November 2015
This is the biggest event of the year for Universal and takes place across both coasts - Hollywood and Orlando and enters its 25th year of horror in 2015. It is an evening extravaganza where as well as experiencing some of the usual attractions, themed haunted houses are open for you to explore, live entertainment is on offer and there are scare zones where "scarectors" roam around to frighten you - these can be anything from zombies to madmen with chainsaws. The theming is absolutely incredible during these events and unlike any other scare attraction in the US.

Details for the 2015 event are extremely limited at this early stage but we do know that Jack the Clown will be returning for the event due to a promotional trailer Universal Orlando has released. Apart from that we have no other details as to the haunted houses on offer in 2015. More information on the 2015 event is not yet available and should be released between July and the end of August 2015.

Halloween Horror Nights (HHN) is very, very popular and *Universal Studios Florida* does get very crowded during these events. Expect to easily wait up to an hour or more in line for each haunted house. This is one time when we highly recommend purchasing the *HHN* Express Pass if you want the full experience and to see everything, though it is an additional supplement of over $100 extra. Alternatively, make multiple visits to see everything on offer.

Dates:
Halloween Horror Nights runs on select nights. Exact dates for 2015 have not yet been announced but Universal Orlando has revealed that the event will run from September 25th to October 31st 2015 making the event shorter than in 2014.

For the 2014 event the event ran on the following dates: September 19th, 20th, 25th, 26th, 27th and 28th, October 2nd, 3rd, 4th, 5th, 9th, 10th, 11th, 12th, 15th, 16th, 17th, 18th, 19th, 22nd, 23rd, 24th, 25th, 26th, 29th, 30th and 31st and November 1st.

Is The Wizarding World of Harry Potter part of HHN?
Halloween Horror Nights will not extend to the Wizarding World of Harry Potter: Diagon Alley area of the park, which will remain closed throughout the events. The area will be opening during normal park hours but will close once *HHN* begins.

However: In 2014, Universal Orlando held a test which meant that guests who were inside Diagon Alley before parking closing and had either a park-to-park ticket OR a *HHN* ticket could remain inside Diagon Alley up to three hours after the park officially closed – as soon as guests exited Diagon Alley they would not be allowed to re-enter. It is unclear whether this system will be re-used in 2015 or even if it will be more widely publicized.

Pricing:
Ticket sales for 2015 are not yet open. For reference, in 2014 a single **general admission ticket** was priced at $95.99 on the gate or it could also be purchased at http://www.halloweenhorrornights.com/orlando/tickets.html in advance. Think this is expensive? We agree, see the other ticket options below.

For online purchases made in advance, the **Rush of Fear** pass was priced at $75.99 and allowed entry at every event night during the first 3 weeks of 2014 for one low price. A **Rush of Fear + HHN Express Pass** option was also available which allowed you entry during the first 3 weeks of 2015 as well as allowing you to bypass the regular lines one time at all the haunted houses, plus participating rides and attractions.

Other advanced purchase options in 2014 included: The **Frequent Fear** pass, which was priced at $86.99 and was valid on September 19th, 20th, 25th, 28th and October 2nd, 5th, 9th, 12th, 15th, 16th, 19th, 22nd, 23rd, 26th, 29th and 30th. The **Frequent Fear + HHN Express Pass** was priced at $194.99 and was valid on the same nights as the regular Frequent Fear Pass, including Express Pass for every night. The **Frequent Fear Plus** was priced at $102.99 and was valid on **September** 19th, 20th, 25th, 26th and 28th, and October 2nd, 3rd, 5th, 9th, 10th, 12th, 15th, 16th, 17th, 19th, 22nd, 23rd, 24th, 26th, 29th, 30th and 31st. The **Frequent Fear Plus + HHN Express Pass** as valid on the same dates as the Frequent Fear Plus pass and was priced at $254.99 – it includes Express Pass access on every night listed. All prices are per person and exclude tax. Annual passholder discounts are available, including for friends and family of passholders. Florida residents and friends can also get HHN ticket discounts.

HHN Express passes:
If you wish to buy separate HHN Express Passes these vary in price from $59.99 to $109.99 per person and are valid during the event night only for haunted houses and attractions. We recommend you buy these in advance as they will sell out for peak nights. On peak nights you NEED a HHN Express Pass to see everything as wait times for haunted houses will be two to three hours so Express Passes are a necessity, not a want. Note that even with an Express Pass you may have to wait up to an hour or more to enter the haunted houses during peak nights – it will not be instant or quick entry. Note that Express Passes purchased for daytime at Universal Orlando are not valid during HHN, nor are the Hotel Express Passes – if you want to skip the lines during HHN you will have to cough up some cash.

HHN as an add on:

In 2014, you could also add a night of Halloween Horror Nights 2014 to your daytime park ticket and save (versus purchasing them separately). Your Halloween Horror Nights ticket did not have to be used the same day as your daytime park ticket. The price in 2014 was $41.99 per person on Sunday through Thursday, $56.99 on Fridays, and $72.99 on Saturdays. Savings varied between $23 and $54. You can buy this in advance with a day ticket, or at the resort itself with a day ticket present with you at the time of purchase.

For reference, in 2014 there were eight different haunted houses – AMC's The Walking Dead, Alien vs. Predator, Dracula Untold, From Dusk Till Dawn, Halloween were all inspired by intellectual properties. There were also three original haunted houses: Dollhouse of the Damned, Giggles & Gore, Inc, Roanoke – Cannibal Colony. Guests can expect the haunted houses to last about 3 to 5 minutes each. Haunted houses for 2015 have not yet been announced.

There were also four scare zones where characters roam the zones causing fear - here you do not need to queue to be scared. In 2014 there were Face Off, The Purge: Anarchy, MASKerade: Unstitched and Bayou of Blood.

As far as live stage shows, 2014 saw the return of Bill & Ted's Excellent Halloween Adventure (a really enjoyable stage show) and there was also a Universal tribute to the Rocky Horror Picture Show.

The following attractions were also open during HHN in 2014: TRANSFORMERS The Ride 3D, Despicable Me Minion Mayhem, Hollywood Rip Ride Rockit, MEN IN BLACK Alien Attack, Revenge of the Mummy and The Simpsons Ride. Queues for attractions are generally non-existent throughout the event as the focus is on the scare aspect of the night for many people. Guests with a HHN Express Pass can use it for both the scare zones and all the aforementioned attractions.

Universal warns that the event "may be too intense for young children and is not recommended for children under the age of 13". Children under this age may come as no proof of age is requested but it is not recommended. This is definitely not a place for children. No costumes or masks are allowed at the event.

RIP Tours (all details for 2014):
You can get a **private VIP tour** (dubbed an 'RIP' tour during HHN) with immediate unlimited access to every haunted house and attraction (plus many other benefits) starting at $1299 for a party of 10, plus the cost of HHN park admission. There are several benefits to this package and if you can get 10 people to do it, $130 each works out at outstanding value for what you get – of course that is the starting price.

If you cannot gather a group, a **public RIP tour** which includes one-time immediate access to every haunted house, plus the attractions (plus many other benefits), starting at $109.99 per person, plus the cost of HHN park admission.

For both experiences you can call for date-specific prices at 1-866-346-9350 or you can email vipexperience@universalorlando.com.

Guided Tours (all details for 2014):
If you want to see how the horror or HHN is created without the scares then Universal Orlando offers several guided tours for you:

- **Unmasking the Horror Tour** – This tour will take you through three haunted houses with the lights on with a guide who will give you a tour as you go through and you will learn about the process that goes into creating these houses. There will be no scares during the tour. Photos are permitted. The tour lasts up to 2 hour 30 minutes for groups of up to 15 guests. Tours are priced at $59.99 per person (plus tax) and there is both a morning and afternoon tour, both tours go through different haunted houses – guests who wish to see all 6 houses on the same day can purchase both tours at a discounted price of $99.99 per person, plus tax. These tours take place during the regular daytime hours of the park.

- **Arcane Insights Tour** – This tour takes place on one of 4 HHN evenings and begins at 7:00 and lasts 6 hours. During the tour you will have a tour guide you, as well as a member of the Universal Orlando Arts and Design Team who will explain everything throughout the tour to do with the creative process. You will experience all of the park's haunted houses, visit a house's makeup and/or wardrobe area and get to take part in a seated Q&A with the member of the Art & Design Team. Pricing is $209.99 per person, plus tax and HHN ticket admission.

For both experiences you can call for date-specific prices at 1-866-346-9350 or you can email vipexperience@universalorlando.com.

How to get in to HHN 45 minutes before everyone else:
Make sure you already have a day ticket or annual pass and are in the park before 4:15pm. The park usually closes at 5:00pm for regular guests on *HHN* and guests are not allowed in after 4:30pm. Make sure you are in one of the lines to enter the *HHN* holding areas - one is near the Revenge of the Mummy and Finnegan's Bar, another is in Springfield USA, another is near Lucy – A Tribute and the fourth is at Diagon Alley. Up to four of these waiting areas may be in operation at once. Make sure you are in line by 4:30pm at the very latest - once you reach the front both your *HHN* and day tickets will be scanned and you will be given a wristband, which allows you enter the waiting area.

You will then wait in this holding area until 5:45pm - do whatever you want to fill the time. At 5:45pm, 45 minutes before *HHN* is scheduled to officially begin you will be allowed into the park once again to explore the *HHN* entertainment including the scare houses - usually only a couple will be open at this time but there will be little or no wait, and you can usually do them all and then explore the others at 6:30pm when *HHN* officially starts!

Our recommended holding area location is the one near the Revenge of the Mummy and Finnegan's Bar as there is a great atmosphere, and places to sit down, as well as places to grab a bite to eat and a drink. Note that these locations may change in 2015 but the Finnegan's Bar location has been a favorite of ours for years.

Chapter 15
Touring Plans:

In order to make the most of your time at the parks we highly recommend you follow one of our touring plans in this guide. These touring plans are *not* designed in order for you to have a leisurely slow day through the parks, they are designed to get as much accomplished in the parks as possible whilst still having fun. This may mean crossing the park back and forth in order to save you from being in long lines but ultimately it will mean that you can get the most out of your Universal Orlando experience. At the moment, the parks do not have a huge amount of attractions meaning that wait times can be long but that it is perfectly possible to do all the rides in a park on the same day with some planning.

Overall, we recommend you spend at least one day at each park, and then use a third or fourth day to do your favorite attractions at both parks, including any you may have missed.

The key to these touring plans is to arrive at the park well before it opens - that means being at the parking lots at least about 60 minutes before park opening if you are driving in. Parking lots open 90 minutes before official park opening hours. If you want to buy tickets on the day (please do not they are much more expensive than buying in advance) then you will need to be at the gates at least 45 minutes before park opening. Otherwise make sure to be at the park gates at least 30 minutes before opening with your park admission in hand. Park gates often open up to 30 minutes before the official opening time.

Using this touring plan: If there is a particular attraction you do not wish to experience simply skip that step and then follow the next one - do not change the order of the steps.

1-Day touring plan for Universal's Islands of Adventure:

Due to the popularity of *The Wizarding World of Harry Potter: Hogsmeade* many guidebooks are recommending you visit this area early on in the day - DON'T! This is what everyone is doing, which means that you end up getting yourself into insanely long lines!

1. Be at the turnstiles with your ticket in hand at least 45 minutes before park opening. Proceed through the gates once they are open. Grab a park map and head straight ahead through the arch and through the *Port of Entry* area of the park. You can come and explore this beautiful area later in the day.
2. When you reach the end of the path you are forced to turn either left or right, turn left and cross the bridge under *The Incredible Hulk Coaster*. Turn right and experience *The Amazing Adventures of Spider-Man*. Lockers are not required for this attraction. Do this before riding *The Hulk* because lines for *Spider-Man* ride built up more quickly, whereas the Hulk's stay constant throughout the day.
3. Walk back to *The Incredible Hulk Coaster* - ride this. Lockers are required for loose items on this ride.
4. Walk back towards *Spider-Man* and ride *Dr. Doom's Fearfall*. Lockers are required for loose items.
5. If all has gone to plan, you should have accomplished all this within the first 45 to 60 minutes of your day.
6. Cross the park to the *Seuss Landing* area. Ride *The Cat in the Hat*. Lockers are not required for this attraction.
7. Ride *Red Fish, Blue Fish, One Fish, Two Fish*. Be prepared to get wet.
8. Now prepare to get absolutely drenched - head to the *Toon Lagoon* area and hit the three water rides just before lunch. *Dudley's Do-Right's Ripsaw Falls* should be first, followed by *Popeye & Bluto's Bilge-Rat Barges*, and finally *Jurassic Park River Adventure*. You will be soaking wet before lunch but most people do these rides after having eaten so you have saved yourself a lot of valuable time in the afternoon. We highly advise eating somewhere outdoors, and not inside in the freezing air-conditioning. Alternatively, make sure you have a change of clothes with you and a rent a locker before experiencing the water rides.

9. Have lunch. In the interests of time we recommend that you dine at a quick service location.
10. If you fit the very limited ride requirements, ride *Pteranodon Flyers*. This will most likely be one of the lengthiest waits of the day due to its extremely low capacity.
11. Head to the *Seuss Landing* are and ride the *High in the Sky Seuss Trolley Train Ride*.
12. Ride the *Caro-seuss-el*. The wait for this should never be above 10 minutes at the very most.
13. Experience the shows: *Poseidon's* Fury (do not wait more than half an hour for this) and *The Eighth Voyage of Sindbad Stunt Show*. If the *Mystic Fountain* is entertaining guests, enjoy that too.
14. Now you only have a few minor rides left to do as well as *The Wizarding World of Harry Potter: Hogsmeade*. Here is where you make your decision - if there are three hours until park closing or more follow the next steps in order. If there are less than 3 hours you may want to head to *The Wizarding World* and follow this touring plan from step number 18.
15. If *Oh, the Stories You'll Hear* is playing in *Seuss Landing*, then watch this show.
16. Explore the *Camp Jurassic* area near *Pteranodon Flyers*.
17. Ride *Storm Force Accelatron*.
18. Head to *The Wizarding World of Harry Potter: Hogsmeade*. Ride *Dragon Challenge*. The wait for this rarely exceeds 30 minutes. Lockers are required for loose items.
19. Ride *Flight of the Hippogriff*.
20. Have dinner - we recommend the *Three Broomsticks* right here in the *Wizarding World*.
21. Experience *Ollivander's Wand Shop*.
22. Ride *Harry Potter and the Forbidden Journey* - Lockers are required for loose items. As long as you are in line even one minute before the park closes they will let you experience the ride. Chances are that within the last hour of the park being open lines for all these experiences and most things throughout the park will be very low and this ride is often a walk-on at this point of the day with no wait in line. Top Tip: A common theme park trick is to keep the posted wait times higher than they really are during the last operating hour of a theme park to trick you into not queuing up for rides. Use your judgment.

1-Day touring plan for Universal Studios Florida:

1. Be at the turnstiles with your ticket in hand at least 45 minutes before park opening. Proceed through the gates. Grab a park map and head straight ahead towards *Despicable Me* on your left hand side. Ride it. If the wait is longer than 30 minutes we would recommend you give this ride a miss due to the time you lose here significantly impacting the remainder of your day.
2. Ride *Transformers: The Ride*. There is a single rider line available. If you find that the line for this ride is already very long then we suggest you skip this step and ride *Transformers* towards the end of the day when queues will be shorter.
3. Ride *Hollywood Rip Ride Rockit*. There is a single rider line available though it is fairly slow moving. Lockers are required for loose items. After this ride you will have done most of the rides with the longest lines in the park.
4. Ride *Revenge of the Mummy*. Lockers are required for loose items. A single rider line is available. We highly recommend the regular queue as the single rider line does not move very quickly and you will miss some of the great theming. Wait times for this ride rarely exceed 30 minutes.
5. Ride *The Simpsons Ride*.
6. Ride *Men in Black: Alien Attack*. A single rider line is available. Lockers are required for loose items.
7. Have lunch. We highly recommend you have a quick service/quick service meal at lunch if you want to maximize your touring time.
8. Watch *Universal's Superstar Parade*. The parade at *Universal Studios Florida* is nowhere near as popular as the parades at Walt Disney World so you should be able to get a front row spot arriving even 10 minutes before the parade starts, especially as the parade route is so long. Often you will even get a front row spot at the parade without stalking out the spot in advance.
9. Ride *E.T. Adventure*. Waits are generally not above 30 minutes.
10. Watch Universal's *Horror Make Up Show*. This is our favorite live show at Universal Orlando. The theatre is fairly small so arrive about 20 minutes before the performance is due to start, to be guaranteed a seat.

11. Watch *Terminator 2: 3D...A Battle Across Time*. This is our other favorite live show at Universal Orlando, and is very different to the *Horror Make Up Show*.
12. Head to *The Wizarding World of Harry Potter: Diagon Alley*. You will want to enter this area *at least* 3 hours before park closing for the full experience. Crowds will be lowest at the end of the day. Ride *Harry Potter and the Escape from Gringotts*, followed by a return journey on the *Hogwarts Express* (note a Park-to-Park ticket is required for access to the Hogwarts Express).
13. Watch the *Universal Cinematic Spectacular*. Views are available from all around the lagoon. We would not be too worried about missing the *Cinematic Spectacular* to get entry into *Diagon Alley* and experience its attractions. We expect crowds will be very high in this area throughout late 2014 and all of 2015.

Important Note: This touring plan does not include all attractions in the park due to time constraints, and because some attractions target younger children such as Barney and *Woody* Woodpecker which may not be suitable for your party. If you have no interest in *The Wizarding World of Harry Potter* it is feasible to do almost all the *other* attractions in this park in a day with careful planning.

Best of both parks 1-day touring plan:

In this touring plan we will detail how to hit the biggest attractions in both parks. It is not feasible to do all attractions at the two parks in just one day, so we have listed the must-dos here. Remember you will need a Universal Park-to-Park ticket to access both parks on the same day. Note that doing the best of both parks in one day has become much more difficult since the addition of *The Wizarding World of Harry Potter: Diagon Alley* and its rides to the Universal Orlando Resort. It is reasonably likely that you will not be able to complete this plan during extremely busy days. This touring plan assumes high crowds and the parks are open until at least 9:00pm. It can also work for lower crowds and shorter opening times.

1. Be at the turnstiles of *Universal Studios Florida* with your ticket in hand before park opening. Be there 45 minutes or more before the park is set to open, as queues build quickly. Proceed through the turnstiles, grab a park map and head straight ahead towards *Despicable Me* on your left hand side. Ride it.
2. Ride *Transformers: The Ride*. Use the single rider line to save time if you can.
3. Ride *Hollywood Rip Ride Rockit*. Use the single rider line to save time if you can. You have now ridden three of the rides with the longest waits in this park.
4. Now be prepared to walk all the way across the park. Ride *The Simpsons Ride*.
5. If it is past 12:30pm at this point, skip this step. Otherwise, Ride *MEN IN BLACK: Alien Attack*.
6. Ride *Revenge of the Mummy*.
7. If it is past 1:45pm at this point, skip this step. Otherwise, Watch the fantastic *Universal Horror Make-Up Show*. Work this around your lunch so either watch it before or after lunch - try to be there 20 minutes early as the theatre is fairly small.
8. Lunch - we recommend *Monsters' Cafe* if you are staying in *Universal Studios Florida* and want a quick meal. Having a table service meal will seriously impede your ability to see the most of both parks in a day.
9. Now it is time for the long walk as you make your way over to the other theme park - *Universal's Islands of Adventure*. Be prepared for long queue lines as this is the busiest point in the day - however lines will still generally be shorter than at *Universal Studios Florida*, which is why we started there.
10. Ride *The Incredible Hulk Coaster*. A single-rider line is sometimes available to speed up entry into the ride if you are willing to use it.
11. If it is past 4:00pm we recommend you skip this step. Otherwise, choose one of the following attractions. Ride *Dudley Do-Right's Ripsaw Falls*, *Popeye & Bluto's Bilge-Rat Barges* or *Jurassic Park River Adventure*. These are all water rides – expect to get soaked.
12. Ride *The Amazing Adventures of Spider-Man*. The queue will be long at this time of day. Use the single rider line if you can to save you a lot of time.
13. Explore *The Wizarding World of Harry Potter: Hogsmeade* - the crowds will probably have lightened by now. Ride

Dragon Challenge, which should not have a wait longer than 30 minutes, especially at this point in the day.

14. Ride *Harry Potter and the Forbidden Journey*. The line should be substantially smaller than in the morning.
15. Catch the *Hogwarts Express* over to *Diagon Alley*. If you are boarding the train 30 minutes or sooner before the park officially closes you will have to move quickly to make it to the final ride.
16. Proceed to *Escape from Gringotts*. This ride may have a long queue (but hopefully not at this time of night) but it should be at the lowest it has been all day. As long as you are in the queue line before park closing you will be able to ride.
17. If time still remains, have dinner somewhere in the *Wizarding World* or elsewhere in the park.

Note: For those staying at on-site hotels, do step 16 then step 15 first at *Universal Studios Florida* using your Early Access privilege and be there before park opening. Then pick up the plan from Step 1 and *Despicable Me*.

Chapter 16

The Future:

The future of Universal Orlando is looking bright with several projects currently in the works - some have been confirmed, others are strong rumors. In this section we cover what will be coming soon to the resort, including the theme parks and what you can look forward to.

In September 2013 Universal's President and Chief Executive Officer, Steve Burke, announced at a conference in California that they plan to open one new attraction per year for the foreseeable future - a pace that no other major theme park can match. This sets an exciting precedent for the future of the resort.

Sapphire Falls Resort Resort – Confirmed (Summer 2016):

A new resort hotel will be coming to the Universal Orlando resort in Summer 2016, bringing the total number of on-site hotels to five. Guests visiting the new Loews Sapphire Falls Resort at Universal Orlando will walk into a colorful Caribbean hideaway built around a lush, tropical lagoon and towering waterfall. Its 1,000 rooms, including 77 suites, will bring the number of on-site hotel rooms at the Universal Orlando resort to 5,200.

A resort-style pool with a water slide, children's play area, sand beach and fire pit will form a central courtyard and will be surrounded by the hotel's guest rooms. There will be water taxi and shuttle access to all of the entertainment and dining options throughout Universal Orlando Resort.

The new hotel will be full service. Amenities will include Early Park Admission to Universal's theme parks, a full-service restaurant with scenic views and outdoor dining, a themed lobby lounge, poolside bar and grill, quick-service marketplace, valet service and a fitness center. This hotel is *not* expected to include complimentary Universal Express Pass unlimited access. Booking information and pricing will be announced at a later date with reservations being accepted from Spring 2015.

Twister to close its doors – Rumor:

In line with the idea that a new attraction will open every year at the Universal Orlando resort, it appears that in early 2015 (January to be precise) *Twister: Ride It Out* will be closing its doors to be replaced by something new. We do not expect the new attraction to be anything major and it may just be a show if it is to open in time for Summer 2015.

King Kong Expansion - Rumor:

A King Kong attraction has long been rumored for *Islands of Adventure* but it looks like it may now be really happening. The area is expected to be a reconstruction of Skull Island and feature one attraction. The attraction is already under construction with a large building now being visible behind the Jurassic Park area of the park – ground work began in Summer 2014. This area is expected to be opened in 2016 for the launch of the new King Kong film due to be released in summer of the same year.

The Lorax Ride / Smurfs Ride - Rumor:

This is yet another rumored expansion for *Islands of Adventure*. An email has been circulated by Universal Orlando asking for feedback on a possible Lorax ride. The character already makes some appearances in the park and there is some logic to the creation of a ride. The ride would be housed in the *Seuss Landing* area of the park. The survey also asked about the possibility of a Smurfs ride which presumably would also be in the same area, or possibly replace *E.T. Adventure* in *Universal Studios Florida*. The survey gave both the ideas of a 3D simulator and a traditional dark ride and asked respondents for their opinions on each. Although this is merely a survey it does give us some indication of what may soon be arriving at the theme parks.

Volcano Bay Water Park – Rumor:
We have stated early in this guide that Universal Orlando is planning some pretty ambitious plans to expand its offerings, and rival the Walt Disney World resort which is only a few miles away. Although Universal already owns the land on which Wet 'n Wild sits, it does not have its own on-site water park with integrated tickets, room charging and other facilities.

This is the reason why it is appears that Universal Orlando is developing its own water park currently entitled 'Volcano Bay'. Rumors states that the park will come in at about 30 acres which is comparable to the size of Wet 'n Wild, and half of the size of the Disney water parks. The park is expected to be located on a plot of land south of the Cabana Bay Beach Resort, with the central icon being a "massive, 200-foot erupting volcano".

There seems to be some credibility to the rumors as popular theme park website Parkscope found a trademark filing for the name 'Volcano Bay' providing "water park rides" as part of its guest services. The same was previously found for a project called "WonderSea" so your guess on the park's final name is as good as ours. As far as the opening date, we will be looking at 2018 at the very earliest in our estimations.

And more...

Universal Orlando also plans to more than triple the number of onsite hotel rooms to between 10,000 and 15,000 in the distant future.

Chapter 17
A Special Thanks:

If you have made it this far, thank you very much for reading everything – we hope this guide has made a big difference to your vacation and you have found some tips that will save you time, money and hassle! Remember to take this guide with you whilst you are on vacation.

To contact us, please use the 'Contact Us' form on our website at http://www.independentguidebooks.com/contact-us/. If you have any corrections, feedback about any element of the guide, or a review of a ride or restaurant - send us a message and we will get back to you! You could even help contribute to the ride and show reviews we will be including in future editions of this guide. To stay up to date on all the latest developments and updates be sure to like our Facebook page at http://www.facebook.com/independentguidebooks/ and sign up to our newsletter on our website (on the right sidebar) at http://www.independentguidebooks.com.

If you have enjoyed this guide you will want to check out **The Independent Guide to Walt Disney World 2015**, **The Independent Guide to Disneyland 2015**, and **The Independent Guide to Disneyland Paris 2015**. Our new guide, **The Independent Guide to Orlando 2015** will be launched in Spring 2015. All of which are available right now! You will find detailed information on every ride, show and attraction and more insider tips that will save you hours in line!

Have fun at Universal Orlando!

Photo credits:
The following photos have been used in this guide under a Creative Commons license.
Thank you to:
- 'Amy' (amyr_81 from Flickr) for the front cover image

- Steve Fishman for the picture of the Universal globe
- Stan Shebs for the photo of Loews Portofino Bay Hotel
- Adam Caudill for the photo of 'Lucy - A Tribute'
- 'Bea&txm' on Flickr for the photo of Dr. Doom's Fearfall
- Joe Shlabotnik for Universal CityWalk
- 'LancerE' on Flickr for AMC Cineplex
- Jeremy Thompson for Blue Man Group, Popeye & Bluto's Bilge-Rat Barges and Animal Actors on Location
- 'Eccentric Scholar' on Flickr for Knockturn alley
- 'The Community – Pop Culture Geek' on Flickr for Ollivander's (Hogsmeade)
- 'zachclarke' on Flickr for Pteranodon Flyers
- Shawn Rossi for the photo of Royal Pacific Resort
- Katy Warner for the photo of the Hard Rock Hotel.
- Wikicommons for many other photos.
- Universal Orlando Resort for photos of the Portofino Bay Hotel, Hogwart's Express, Cabana Bay Beach Resort, the Diagon Alley waterfront and Escape from Gringotts.

CPSIA information can be obtained at www.ICGtesting.com
Printed in the USA
BVOW04s0133100215

387087BV00004B/25/P